ready,

aim,

specialize!

ready, aim, specialize!

Create Your Own Writing Specialty and *MAKE MORE MONEY!*

Kelly James-Enger

Marion Street Press, Inc.
Oak Park, Illinois

Cover design by Rick Menard

ISBN 978-1-933338-24-8
Printed in U.S.A.
Printing 10 9 8 7 6 5 4 3 2 1

Marion Street Press, Inc.
PO Box 2249
Oak Park, IL 60303
866-443-7987
www.marionstreetpress.com

For Erik and Ryan, my favorite boys

Contents

Section 3: Growing Your Writing Business

Acknowledgments

No writer works in a vacuum, and so I'd like to acknowledge a number of people. First, my editor, Ed Avis of Marion Street Press, who agreed to resurrect this book in an updated edition. As a result, I was able to add material to make it even more helpful, especially for new freelancers. Thanks too to Diana Gerardi, who enables me to work by taking such good care of my baby boy, and proofreads for me as well. Special thanks to my favorite blonde, Cindy, and to Erik.

Finally, thanks to all the writers who graciously shared their experience, advice and wisdom for this edition of Ready, Aim, Specialize: Susanne Alexander, Linda Wasmer Andrews, Cathy Wilkinson Barash, Tom Bedell, Chuck Bednar, Cindy BeMent, Monica Bhide, Judy Bistany, Bob Bittner, Ed Blonz, Chris Bonney, Melanie Bowden, Tom Brosnahan, Jill S. Browning, Polly Campbell, Salvatore Caputo, Sharon Cindrich, Andrea Cooper, Monique Cuvelier, Jackie Dishner, Lain Ehmann, Debbie Elicksen, Leslie Gilbert Elman, Linda Formichelli, Helen Gallagher, Ed Gordon, Susan J. Gordon, Sam Greengard, Tim Harper, Diane Benson Harrington, Leah Ingram, Lisa Iannucci, Joshua Karp, Mary Beth Klatt, Kathy Landis, Kathryn Lay, Joan Lisante, Margaret Littman, Diana Luger, Megan McMorris, Robert Mark, W. Eric Martin, Janet Mazur, JoAnn Milivojevic, Tommy Newcomb, Melba Newsome, Kristin Ohlson, Susan Kutchin Pallant, Ari Tye Radetsky, Kristin Baird Rattini, Kelly Boyer Sagert, Kathy Sena, Erik Sherman, Deborah Shouse, Debbie Simler-Goff, Michelle Sussman, Thomas Trimingham, Claire Walter, and Alida Zamboni.

Introduction

Want to make more money and set yourself apart from other free-lance writers? Specialize.

That's the theory behind this book, which grew out of my own experience as a fulltime freelancer. Once I developed a specialty of my own (several of them, actually), I found that assignments came easier, my productivity increased, and my income quadrupled—all because I concentrated on a handful of subjects rather than trying to write about anything and everything.

But specializing isn't only for experienced writers. Pitching story ideas that you already have a background in or experience with can help new writers get their first assignments and launch their freelance careers. To help you learn why you should—and how you can—specialize as a freelancer, this book is divided into three sections:

Section One: Getting Started serves as an overview. Chapter 1 explains why you should consider specializing; Chapter 2 shows you how to do it. In chapter 3, you'll learn how to write a query letter, and see actual samples of queries by new freelancers that sold, while chapter 4 reviews effective marketing and research techniques. Finally, chapter 5 provides an overview of the article-writing process from developing the kernel of an idea to seeing your work appear in print.

Section Two: The Top Ten Hottest Specialties includes ten chapters, each dedicated to a particular nonfiction writing specialty. Chapters 6 through 15 give a brief introduction to each of these niches, strategies for coming up with ideas, practical advice from writers who work in these areas, potential markets for articles, a sample query that sold, and organizations, websites, books, and other helpful resources. Each chapter also includes a "Tale from the Front"—"dos" and "don'ts" from a successful freelancer in this area.

Section Three: Growing your Writing Business includes two chapters that describe how to branch out into other fields and maximize your income and productivity. A brief appendix includes books, organizations, and market sources as well.

I realize every writer has his or her own reasons for freelancing. Even if you just want to get into print, why not make some money—or more money—from your words as well? This book will help you do that, whether you've been published already or still want to break into print. Read on for ways that you expand your writing career—by narrowing your focus.

Section One: Getting Started

Narrowing Your Focus: Why Specialize?

Guess what? You're a specialist already. You just may not know it yet. Simply by living your life up until now, you've learned about a variety of subjects. Chances are you've worked a number of jobs, probably in different industries. You've had relationships with people—family, coworkers, lovers, friends. You've taken classes, maybe obtained a college degree or two. You've overcome obstacles. You've explored hobbies. You've developed interests, likes, dislikes, opinions, goals and dreams.

Each of us has a unique history and life experience. If you'd like to break into print, why not harness that experience to break into the freelance world?

I've been a fulltime freelance journalist for more than a decade now, and I've been teaching magazine writing and speaking at writers' conferences and other events throughout the United States for almost as long. I've helped hundreds of new writers get published for the first time, helped seasoned writers break into more lucrative markets, and helped writers of all experience levels work more efficiently and make more money as a result.

All by suggesting one thing: that they specialize.

Let me make something clear. Specializing doesn't prevent you from writing about anything you want to. You still have that option. It does mean that you focus on your unique strengths and background, especially as a new writer. Specializing can get you into print. And over time, it can transform a so-so freelance career into one that lets you reach your dreams and monetary goals.

Starting Out

Imagine that you're an editor at a magazine. Unless you're a major name like Anna Wintour or Tina Brown, chances are you're overworked and underpaid. One of your many tasks is assigning stories to fill the pages of your magazine. Every issue. No matter what.

That's the bad news. The good news is you've got no shortage of free-lancers to help you do it. In fact, you receive hundreds, maybe thousands of queries a month. Some are from experienced writers; many more are from "newbies" with little in the way of clips or experience. Whom do you choose to work with?

The writer who you believe can deliver the story. And all things being equal, would you rather assign this piece to a freelancer who's new to the subject, or the one who already has experience with it?

The answer is clear. That's why I suggest that new or inexperienced writers start by pitching stories they are "uniquely qualified" to write. In the next chapter, I'll help you identify a slew of areas that you can claim a background in, but for now, let me explain why this is essential, especially for your first queries.

Throughout this book, you'll find 20 queries that resulted in assignments. For now, just keep in mind that a query includes four basic parts:

1) The lead, which is designed to catch the editor's attention. It might be a startling statistic, a recent study result, a timely news event, or an anecdote. The key is that it interests the editor enough to continue reading.

2) The "why write it" section. This paragraph (or two, if you have a particularly detailed query) fleshes out the idea, demonstrating why the readers of the magazine will be interested in the topic.

3) The "nuts and bolts" paragraph. Here you give the details of the story itself. What types of sources will you contact? How long will the story be? Will it have sidebars, and if so, how many? What section of the magazine will the story fit in? What's the working title?

4) The "I-am-so-great" paragraph (or "ISG"). Here, you highlight your relevant qualifications, including your writing experience and background with the subject matter. This is the paragraph where you showcase your unique qualifications and convince the editor to give you the assignment.

14

Let me give you a few examples of compelling I-am-so-great paragraphs from early in my freelance career:

When I pitched a story on a hidden dating treasure (also known as "shy guys"), I made sure that I mentioned that I am an extrovert who fell in love with and married a shy guy. ("10 Reasons to Date a Shy Guy," *Complete Woman*, October/November, 1997.)

I pitched a true-life feature about a young woman's struggle with a serious, debilitating yet undiagnosed medical problem to a number of women's magazines. In my ISG, I wrote that I had already spoken with the woman and had her permission to write her story. ("An Answer at Last," *Woman's World*, April 7, 1998.)

When I queried a bridal magazine with a story idea on the importance of communicating about money, I included an anecdotal lead about a money argument between newlyweds. In my ISG, I revealed that the couple was me and my newlywed husband. ("A Match Made in Financial Heaven," *Bridal Guide*, March/April, 1998.)

But the ISG isn't only for new writers. As I've garnered experience in a variety of subject areas, I've harnessed it to break into new markets as well as other types of writing. For example:

When sending a letter of introduction to *IGA Grocergram*, a trade magazine for grocery store owners, I neglected to include that I'd recently worked part-time at Trader Joe's, a specialty grocery store. But when I followed up with editor by phone, you better believe I worked that fact into the conversation!

When contacting Pampered Chef about freelancing for their corporate communications department, I mentioned my relevant experience writing about food and nutrition for national magazines. (I'm not a big cook; otherwise, I would have said so.)

When sending a letter of introduction to a medical consulting firm, I mentioned both my health-writing background and my work (even though it had been years prior) doing PR for a small hospital.

Get it? The idea is to always look for some connection you have with the work you're pitching, even if it's a tenuous one.

Walking the Walk

Let me confess something: I didn't start out as a freelancer understanding the importance of a powerful ISG. I learned the hard way, sending out hundreds of queries that were rejected. I would pitch any and every idea, regardless of how much I knew about the subject—and my sketchy, poorly conceived queries reflected that. So did my annual income.

I started freelancing fulltime on January 1, 1997. I was a lawyer in my former life, and during the last year of practice, I'd been diligent about sending out articles for publication. (I knew so little about the publishing business I didn't even realize freelancers sent query letters. I wrote articles, mailed them in, and hoped. Not an effective way of working, by the way.) But I did manage to sell two articles in 1996—the first to *Cosmopolitan*, the second to *BRIDE'S*.

Those two sales gave me the confidence to quit. I remember thinking that I'd finally found a way out of the law. I'd quit my job and free-lance for magazines for money while I wrote my novel. (I'd been accumulating a stash of short stories and unfinished novels in my 20s, all of which featured unhappy female lawyers. Yet they were all fiction, of course.)

But to be honest, I had no idea of what I was getting into. Although I'd majored in rhetoric in college and fantasized about "being a writer" for most of my life, I had no working knowledge of the freelance lifestyle. At the time I escaped the law, I had never spoken to or even a seen a "freelance writer" (at least not to my knowledge) and had no concept of what exactly self-employed writers did all day—other than write, of course.

I was, however, extremely motivated. Although I'd managed to scrimp together six months' worth of cash to live on, I knew I'd have to nail paying assignments immediately to be able to continue doing it full-time. I also knew I didn't want to go back to practicing law. That gave me six months to get my writing career off the ground.

As a result, I was always as concerned with my bottom line as I was with the quality of my writing. I'd written short fiction and poetry for years, but I'd already figured out there were few high-paying markets for this kind of writing. My success selling the two articles to *Cosmopolitan* and *BRIDE'S* made me believe that freelancing fulltime would be a snap. (Um, not quite.)

Remember, I knew nothing about the rules of the game—like that you were supposed to write queries first. I churned out articles on a variety of topics and dashed them off to magazines that seemed to fit the subject matter and tone. I read everything I could about freelancing and quickly realized that I needed to be writing queries rather than articles—which saved a tremendous amount of time and also increased my article sale rate.

Writing as a sideline had netted me a couple of decent checks, but if I was going to write full-time, I needed a financial goal to shoot for. My first year, it was a modest one—$10,000. I still can't remember why I chose that figure other than the fact that it was a nice, neat sum. If I could make $10,000 from freelancing my first year, I thought, then maybe I could succeed in this new career I'd chosen.

But while I had this dollar figure as my goal, I didn't concern myself with how I would achieve it. My so-called strategy was to query madly, let everyone I could think of know that I was a fulltime freelancer, and take every writing assignment that came my way—provided it paid. And I did just about everything my first year. I wrote brochures for local companies for a few hundred dollars. I "strung" (in the newspaper biz, freelancers are often called stringers) for the local paper and produced features that paid between $35 and $75, and wrote real estate "advertorials" (sales pieces that described specific properties) for $50 each. I took on an educational consulting job where I produced career materials and spoke to grade school students about their future jobs, and did copywriting for a local hospital for $35/hour. In the meantime, I queried magazines with story ideas and occasionally sent out essays and completed articles as well.

When it came to magazines, my approach at the time was to look for story ideas and then find the appropriate markets for those articles. In between dozens of rejections, magazine assignments trickled in. *BRIDE'S* assigned me another piece, this one on combining two households into one when you marry. *Vegetarian Times* asked me to write a 600-word story on creating a local vegetarian group. *Complete Woman* bought my light piece on 10 reasons to date "shy guys." I wrote about a unique high school paper for *Editor & Publisher,* and about a martial arts expert who teaches self-defense classes to people with physical limitations for *Accent on Living. The Lion* asked me to cover a charity car show sponsored by the local Lions club after I pitched the idea to them.

What made these ideas—the ones that were actually assigned—different from the ones that were rejected? In retrospect, I realize that I had a unique connection or background with all of the successful pitches. I'd recently combined two households when I married my husband. I knew a local woman who'd started her own local vegetarian group. I'd come across the unique high school paper at a conference, and I'd contacted the martial arts expert about doing a story after I read about him in the local paper. As for the Lions car show? It was held in my town every year—who better than me to write about it? And you've already heard about my affection for shy guys.

So far, so good. I was learning the importance of the ISG, even if I didn't call it that yet. But during this time, I had no intention of specializing in any particular area. I wrote about any idea that I thought would fit a particular market and bring me some cash. It didn't matter to me if I was writing about charity car shows, one-on-one marketing techniques or animal research; I only cared about the assignment, the clip, and the check—and rightly so. With my limited experience, I couldn't afford to be too choosy about work. I needed to build my portfolio and gain experience—after all, I had <u>no journalism background</u> and was basically learning the ropes by trial and error.

Creating a Niche...by Accident

But there were tradeoffs. Although I was slowly amassing clips, I was also spending hours and hours reviewing possible magazine markets, researching potential story ideas, and writing compelling query letters. I might spend a day or more gathering information and writing up a query which would then be rejected; in the meantime, I was busily pitching as many magazines as I possibly could. At one point, I had 54 query letters, completed articles, and essays circulating in the mail. But from a percentage standpoint, not many of these queries or articles were selling.

This is what I now call the "saturation bombing technique"—simply sending out as many articles and queries as you can manage. You figure, hey, if I get enough stuff out there, something will happen.

I fell victim to this belief early on. I'd lie in bed at night, scanning *Writer's Market* for "$$$$" (which signifies a high-paying magazine). If a magazine paid well (and sadly, that was often my only consideration), I'd whip up a query or an article, often without even bothering to look at the magazine itself. Guess what? Though I sent out hundreds of queries the first couple of years, I've never sold to a market that I didn't actually read first—even though I could have easily acquired a sample issue from the publisher simply by writing and requesting a copy. Today, it's even easier—most publications have websites that provide writers with an easy way to check content and tone. Better yet, many list their writers' guidelines online as well.

The end result of all this work for little payoff was burnout—within the first eight months of my fledgling writing career. I was working mornings, afternoons, evenings, and most weekends—pretty much the same way I had as a lawyer, except that I was making hardly any money. Researching so many different types of story ideas and trying to keep up with dozens of different markets was taking its toll. I was tired, cranky, discouraged, and rapidly losing enthusiasm for the idea of "being a writer." There had to be an easier way.

It turned out there was. Rather than trying to cover a wide variety of subjects, I started to concentrate on a handful of topics that interested me and were a part of my life—health, fitness, nutrition, and relationships—and began developing a specialty in those areas.

In the years since then, I've met hundreds of other freelance writers, and have discovered that the majority of the ones who make a good living freelancing fulltime (say, more than $50,000 a year) have created niches for themselves. Maybe they write about fitness and health. Or business and technology. Or food and nutrition. Or home and garden. Rather than being generalists, they're now specializing in specific areas, and reaping the benefits of doing so. As you'll see in the pages and chapters to come, creating a nonfiction specialty can enable you to:

Get more assignments, even as an inexperienced writer
Command higher per-word rates
Develop and pitch timely story ideas more efficiently
Save time researching and writing articles
Position yourself as an expert and build a platform
Obtain assignments from higher-paying markets
Develop relationships with editors
Create an inventory of stories for reprinting and reselling
Branch into other types of writing (such as books and corporate work)
Break into new subject areas

My first specialty came about quite by accident. After selling two articles to *BRIDE'S*, I'd developed a list of other possible wedding-related story ideas. When *BRIDE'S* turned them down, I pitched some of them to *Bridal Guide*. Based on my clips and ideas, the editor at *Bridal Guide* assigned one. That led to another story for that magazine, and then another; in the meantime, I queried some of the remaining rejected ideas to *For the Bride by Demetrios* and started picking up assignments there as well. In a matter of months, I'd turned two bridal articles into a specialty of sorts. I took my current life situation—I was engaged, then a newlywed—and mined it for story ideas. Since then, I've written more than 30 stories for bridal magazines, many of which have been reprinted at least once, and have been a contributing editor at *For the Bride* for the last five years. And now that I've created a name for myself as a bridal writer, it doesn't matter that I'm closing in on my 10-year anniversary.

From Fat to Fit: Another Niche is Created

I've been interested in fitness and nutrition topics since college, partly due to the fact that I managed to gain a whopping 45 pounds my freshman year. (This was the period my mother euphemistically refers to as "when there was more of you to love.") I'd been a competitive swimmer in high school, and ate to fuel myself for long workouts. When I started college, I quit swimming—but kept eating the way I had before. When I realized I had outgrown my summer clothes, I started running and counting calories to lose the extra weight, which led to a long-standing interest in nutrition and exercise. Over the years, I've continued to run regularly and I still manage to hit the gym a couple of times a week to lift weights or cross-train.

My first fitness-related sale was to *Shape*; I pitched a story on how to maintain your fitness routine when you relocate. Because I'd moved four times in five years, I was uniquely qualified to write the piece, and I incorporated my first-hand experience into the lead. That clip helped me get my first assignment for *Fit* on how to determine your exercise personality. This soon led to other articles for my editor there on topics including exercise addiction, easy ways to eat better, and potential dieting dangers. In the meantime, I pitched new story ideas to *Fitness* and wrote a number of workout articles for that publication as well.

Although I hadn't intended to specialize in fitness and diet topics, it was starting to pay off. First, I was finding it easier to come up with story ideas because I was writing about subjects that interested and directly affected me. My own experiences and that of friends and family often inspired article ideas. After I broke my ankle and had to take six weeks off from running, I turned to a heart-rate monitor to help me get back in shape. That turned into a story ("Target your Training" *Fit*). My sister-in-law was diagnosed with sleep apnea after fighting fatigue for months. That turned into a story. ("Tired of being Tired?" *Woman's Day*) After I was forced to wait 10 minutes to use an abdominal machine at the gym (this woman refused to relinquish her seat!), I realized I had the perfect lead for a query—and that turned into a story as well ("The Top Ten Gym Sins," *Fit*)!

The second advantage was that I was spending less time researching these topics. For example, when writing an exercise story, I knew what the personal trainer meant when she talked about a move designed to target your "lats." When a physician quoted a figure from the "CDC," I knew he meant the U.S. Centers for Disease Control. And if a dietitian mentioned the benefits of consuming omega-3 fats, I didn't have to ask what exactly those were. The more I wrote about these topics, the deeper my knowledge became and the easier it was to research and compose the final stories. I was also developing a Rolodex of experts to whom I could turn for interviews or when I just needed to quickly confirm a fact or nab a quote.

Megan McMorris has worked as an editor at magazines including *Fit* and *Fitness*; she's now a freelancer based in Portland, Oregon, whose stories have appeared in magazines including *Fitness, Self, Sports Illustrated for Women, Woman's Day,* and *Glamour.* She says her lifelong interest in fitness was the jumping-off point for her magazine writing and editing career, and agrees there are many benefits to having a writing niche.

"For one thing, after doing so many fitness-related articles, I feel like I've become somewhat of a 'mini' expert myself, and therefore I don't have to research nearly as much as I would if the topic is completely foreign to me, which makes it easier," says McMorris. "Another pro to having a niche is that when I get an assignment, I already have plenty of contacts in the fitness field, many of whom remember me from previous articles, so it's very easy to get interviews. I don't have to spend time researching who the top experts are, because I already know them." Her knowledge of fitness-related topics has also helped her get first-time assignments from magazines she hasn't written for before. In fact, many editors approach her with article opportunities, and her expertise has led to books as well, including *Oregon Hiking* (Foghorn Outdoors, 2004) and *Pacific Northwest Hiking* (Foghorn Outdoors, 2005).

Getting More Green: The Financial Payoff

Specializing improved my query success rate, which resulted in a major increase in income. It makes sense—I was writing fewer queries, but they were more likely to result in assignments. As I established myself as a freelancer with a background in fitness and later in health and nutrition, I also became more valuable to the editors I worked for. In addition to getting more assignments, my average per-word rates started to rise. One magazine that had paid me 50 cents/word agreed to raise my rate to 75 cents/word, which meant an additional $250 for a 1,000-word article. Another boosted my fee from $1 to $1.25/word. A third offered me $1.35/word for my first health story because the editor knew I'd written other fitness and health-related articles. Most markets are willing to pay more to writers who come equipped with a background in the area they're writing about.

Just ask corporate pilot and freelancer Rob Mark of Evanston, Illinois, who first started writing about aviation subjects. However, he quickly realized that knowing about related areas would make him a more effective researcher and writer. He spent time learning about business, marketing, and technology subjects to help set him apart from other freelancers. "When someone starts talking about something on an aviation story that is very business-focused, for example, you need to be conversant enough in that language that you can talk the talk," says

Mark. "I think when the person you're interviewing realizes that you can either speak or understand some of the lingo that is important to them, it puts them at ease. And if you have some experience in these areas, you can ask biting questions you might not even think of if you didn't know a whole lot about business or technology."

Mark's experience has also allowed him to negotiate higher rates for many articles. "When you have editors who can just give you the story and let you run with it, that shows a lot of confidence and certainly speaks to the issue of where they place you on their writer hierarchy," says Mark. "And in some cases it's allowed me to pull more money out of certain stories because they know I can do that." It makes sense. If the editor knows that you'll do a good job, it saves them hassles and headaches, which is usually worth a few more dollars to them.

Another benefit of specializing is that it enables writers to break into markets that might otherwise be closed to them. For example, I hadn't written for any parenting magazines but I wanted to break into this field. What did I do? Pitch some women's health ideas to an editor at *Parents*. I used a similar approach—suggesting a variety of health and fitness-related story ideas—to query *RxRemedy*, a now defunct publication aimed at 50+ readers. Both stories were assigned, not because I fit the reader profile, but because of my health writing experience.

More Than One Hat: Multiple Specialties

Just because you specialize doesn't mean you're limited to one field. Linda Formichelli, a freelancer in Concord, New Hampshire, says that she has multiple niches which include business, health/nutrition, career, pets, and writing-related articles. "I seem to have fallen into each of these niches. Once I sold a single article in one of these areas, I was able to use that article as a clip to get more work in the field," says Formichelli. "The reason that I have so many niches is that when I brainstorm ideas, I'm not constrained by field—I'm all over the place! In one session I may come up with an idea for *Wired* and an idea for *Family Circle*, both of which I've written for.

"I have so many niches that I consider myself a generalist. But within each of those niches, I find it easier to get work because I can show editors plenty of clips to prove that I know my stuff," she continues. "Those clips also make it easier to get into the top magazines in each niche, so I earn higher rates."

Kristin Baird Rattini, a freelancer who spent four years in Shanghai, China before settling in Howell, New Jersey, turned a one-time opportunity into ongoing work assignments from a number of corporate magazines. "The old 'who you know' got me my break into corporate publications. A high school friend was communications director for a Midwestern telecommunications company," says Rattini. "She needed new writers for the company's quarterly in-house magazine, so she called. Those clips helped me land work with Pohly & Partners custom publications, *True Value, IGA Grocergram*, and *Correspondent*, a magazine put out by Aid Association for Lutherans."

Rattini didn't intend to develop another niche in consumer finance, but had queried the Credit Union National Association with her corporate clips. "The editor liked my style, so she gave me work on CUNA's consumer finance publications," says Rattini. "Over the next three years I landed several dozen assignments with CUNA, which in turn led to stories for *Family Circle* and other larger publications. I've since become well-versed on credit cards, mortgages, investing and other consumer finance topics."

Yet Rattini doesn't limit herself to these stories. She has taken advantage of her time in Shanghai to do more travel writing, and her stories about China have appeared in in-flight magazines for Continental and American airlines as well as Fodor's travel guidebooks. "Having more than one niche proves several things to prospective editors," she says. "My clips not only show the depth of my experience in these given niches, but they also prove that I'm both a versatile writer and a thorough researcher to be able to write well on such varied topics."

Remember, specializing doesn't mean you're limited to only a handful of subject areas. It's more about presenting yourself as an expert, or at least as someone who has more experience than the average person, to potential clients. "There are SCUBA diving magazines that know me as a scuba writer. There are food magazines that know me as a food writer. There are business magazines that know me as a business writer, and technology magazines that know me as a tech writer," says Erik Sherman of Colrain, Massachusetts. "It's a matter, sometimes, of creating the perception that will aid the sale."

That's an excellent strategy to remember: create the perception that will aid the sale. If you're a relatively inexperienced writer, pitch ideas that you have some kind of background in. If you already have some clips to your name, highlight whatever experience puts you in the best light to an editor. That may mean that you've written about the subject before; that you've done extensive research on the topic; that you have access to compelling sources for the story; or that you've found a fresh way to approach an evergreen subject. When you highlight your unique background, experience, or connections in your ISG, you make it easy for an editor to give you an assignment.

In the chapters that follow, you'll explore some of the hottest and highest-paying nonfiction specialties and learn how to turn your unique background and experience into one or more specialties, increasing your freelance income in the process. You'll discover the "dos" and "don'ts" of writing about each area from freelancers who cover those topics, and get an idea of the types of markets that buy and publish these kinds of stories. And you'll find organizations, associations, websites and other resources that will be invaluable as you begin to carve out one or more specialties of your own.

Choosing Your Weapon(s): Select Your Specialty

So, what does it take to create a specialty? At the outset, nothing more than some background in the subject—or better yet, personal experience with the topic you're pitching. As I said in chapter 1, it's likely that you already know a significant amount (or at least more than the average person) about a number of subjects. I suggest you capitalize on that knowledge to help you get your first assignments—or, if you're more experienced, to focus your writing career on several areas to make you more efficient in your work.

Contrary to what you might think, you needn't be an M.D. or other recognized "expert" to focus your writing in a particular area. Your educational background, life experience, and interest in certain subjects can all be translated into a writing-related specialty. When I teach magazine writing, I have students write down at least five things about their lives that they have specialized knowledge or interest in. Make a list of your own to get you started thinking about what you bring to the table when you pitch a story, and don't stop at five—the more subject areas you can come up with, the better.

For example, have you traveled the world? Lived in different parts of the United States? Raised children—or are raising them now? Dealt with a chronic medical condition? Are you an avid gardener? Do you cook from scratch and have the ability to whip up fantastic dinners in 30 minutes' time? Do you run your own business? Do you have first-hand knowledge of a particular industry, trade or profession? What are your hobbies? Have you volunteered for a church, school or nonprofit organization? Who are your friends, family members, co-workers and colleagues? What sorts of specialized knowledge do they have? What experiences have they had, or are they having, that might turn into story ideas?

Use this space to create a list of your own:

I have specialized knowledge about the following subjects:

_____

_____

_____

_____

My work experience includes the following subjects:

_____

_____

_____

_____

My hobbies and interests include the following:

_____

_____

_____

_____

I know or have access to people who have expertise in the following areas:

_____

_____

_____

_____

I'm interested in the following subjects:

_____

_____

_____

_____

I'm currently dealing with these issues (at work, at home, in your personal life):

_____

_____

_____

_____

I'm passionate about the following subjects:

_____

_____

_____

_____

I've experienced these life-changing events (e.g. parenthood, divorce, disease):

_____

_____

_____

_____

In the last year, I've accomplished the following:

_____

_____

_____

_____

Creating a list of these subjects will often trigger story ideas and will also give you an idea of the many areas in which you have a background that other writers may not. For example, when I created a list of my own as an example in a recent writing workshop, I came up with the following:

- My dad is a dentist, and I worked for him before I went to law school
- I've been a runner for twenty years
- I've had back problems off and on for the same twenty years
- I'm an adoptive parent
- I'm on my second (and hopefully last) marriage

Even a cursory look at this list proves that I do have specialized knowledge I can use when pitching and writing articles. I've had personal experience that many people have not. If I were a new writer, with no experience or clips, I'd be better off pitching an article on adopting, running, or even back problems than pitching a story on a subject I know nothing about.

In fact, my interest in running has led to a slew of story ideas, both today and at the beginning of my writing career. Early on, I wrote about using heart-rate monitors to train, the importance of stretching for flexibility, how to maintain your exercise motivation, and how your eating habits can help you get more out of your workouts. Recently I've written about topics including how to avoid running-related injuries, how to be your own fitness coach, and how to launch a regular walking/running program. While I don't have a degree in exercise physiology or sports medicine, my longstanding interest in running and fitness give me a depth of knowledge that the average writer simply doesn't have. Can I call it a specialty? Sure.

Most freelancers break into the field by pitching subjects that they're familiar with, and that proved true for me as well. My first article sale was to *Cosmopolitan* magazine. I wrote a service-oriented piece about how to survive your "last two weeks" at a job after you've given your notice. I had first-hand experience with this subject—as an unhappy lawyer, I had changed firms several times during my short career, each time hoping the new job would be the right fit for me.

My friends and I had also commiserated about the misery of those final days—you know you don't want to be there, and they know you don't want to be there. It's a tense, uncomfortable experience for nearly everyone. Many times during those last two weeks, I had to bite my tongue from saying things like "you'll miss me when I'm gone" or "you have no idea how much I've hated working here," or similar bridge-burning comments. I figured other *Cosmo* readers would relate to this topic…and they did.

My legal background also gave me the idea for my second published article—a story for *BRIDE'S* on how engaged couples can avoid legal problems as they plan their weddings. I was engaged at the time I wrote it, and was amazed at how many unscrupulous vendors I ran into. Several reception hall owners, for example, dodged questions about how much liability insurance they carried, and two refused to put bids in writing. One particularly sleazy guy even told me that I "didn't need to worry myself about things like that." Little did he know that as a contract lawyer, I was paid to worry about "things like that." Fortunately I knew better than to hire any of these winners, but I also realized how easily another bride could be—and often is—taken advantage of in this situation.

The eventual article, "Promises, Promises," gave engaged couples practical ways to protect themselves and avoid potential legal problems, drawing on my experience both as an attorney and as a bride. The editor who bought it told me that I'd done a good job of dispensing legal advice in straightforward, easy-to-understand language. "Most of the articles we get from attorneys and accountants are way too complicated and full of legalese and jargon," she said. "But yours is perfect for our audience."

Different Strokes for Different Folks: The Decision to Specialize

Some life experiences naturally lend themselves to a slew of article ideas. Parenting is one such area. Janet Mazur, a freelancer in Ocean Grove, New Jersey, was a former newspaper reporter and a magazine writer/editor in the United States. She'd also freelanced while living abroad and had worked for major daily papers in Sydney and Melbourne, Australia, writing general features. But she never gave parenting writing a thought until she became a parent herself.

"It seemed a logical transition," says Mazur. "And frankly, I've written partially for selfish purposes when it comes to parenting. There are so many things I wanted to know and explore…as a new mom, at home by choice, I yearned to connect with other women in the same boat." Mazur's first parenting story was a feature for a newspaper on how new moms could hook up with each other. The story addressed their desire for connection, the unexpected loneliness of staying at home with a new baby, and the depression women sometimes experience as a result.

Since then, Mazur has found both her daughters to be an inexhaustible supply of story ideas. "It is one of the unexpected bonuses of having children and being a writer—a gift, really," says Mazur. "They are an easy source, an endless well of ideas, because they change and grow all the time. Their 'issues' are always in flux."

For example, when her older daughter was a toddler with a "blankie," Mazur wrote a story explaining the purpose of comfort objects, using her child as the lead. As her daughter grew, Mazur wrote about developmental issues like spitting up and skin ailments, and later produced articles aimed at parents of school-aged kids—like what to do when your child starts hanging out with the neighborhood "bad kids." Today, Mazur is a fulltime writing teacher at The College of New Jersey, but still occasionally covers parenting subjects.

Mazur already had clips and experience before she started covering parenting topics, but writing about parenting and child care is a great way for new writers to gain experience. Sharon Cindrich of Wauwatosa, Wisconsin was a stay-at-home mom who launched her freelance career when her children were young. She started writing and sending out essays, only to have them rejected. After taking a class in essay writing, she polished her skills and sold her first piece to the "Woman News" section of *The Chicago Tribune*.

Since then, she's sold dozens of essays and now is a regular columnist for *West Suburban Living*, a regional magazine. She also writes articles for a variety of magazines and newspapers, but has chosen to focus on family, health, and parenting issues. "It's always easier. I'm already an expert of sorts because most of the things I write about are issues in my own life," says Cindrich, author of *E-Parenting: Keeping up With Your Tech-Savvy Kids* (Random House, 2007.) "Because of that, I can reach people and pass on information more effectively than if I didn't know it as well."

If you're a new writer, consider using your experience in a particular industry as a stepping stone to getting published. Joan Lisante, an attorney and freelancer based in Oakton, Virginia, started her freelance career by publishing a humorous essay on what she calls "real-life Barbies" in several newspapers. She realized her legal background gave her a unique perspective that she could sell to editors when pitching business and legal-related topics. For a time, she specialized in writing about business and legal topics, eventually branching out to cover medical, technical, and teen/young adult issues as well.

Some writers choose to specialize at the outset to set themselves apart from others in the field. Melba Newsome, a freelancer in Charlotte, North Carolina was working fulltime as a paralegal in Los Angeles when she decided to start writing. She found the process frustrating at first. "I kept getting rejected or heard nothing back at all. I got absolutely nowhere sending out service or health ideas," says Newsome. "Then I pitched true life stories. I got my first assignment for a national magazine (*Family Circle*) with a true life story. I realized that I had much better batting average with these types of stories."

Newsome decided to focus on finding the stories that editors wouldn't be able to come up with on their own. "It was clear that so many of the lifestyle or general interest ideas were generated in-house. But there was no one at the editorial meetings saying, 'I have a great story about a woman who was in a harem for 6 months!'" she explains. "They needed writers on the ground and outside of New York for that. That was me!" In the years since then, she's written dozens of true-life stories for magazines including *Cosmopolitan, Marie Claire, Essence, Good Housekeeping,* and *Family Circle.* The fact that she's willing to do some digging and come up with unique stories has kept her in demand.

"Editors want writers who can generate a steady stream of ideas. It saves them time and a lot of hassle," says Newsome. "I try and set myself apart by finding the greatest story subjects. Of course, this means watching a lot of trash TV and reading a lot of sleazy stories. One editor told me that I was the exception by far. I was one of the few writers they had who came up with their own ideas. Most of them were generated in-house which meant they were constantly brainstorming and scrambling for ideas. Having someone say, 'here are three stories' makes her life easier."

Specializing Later On

If you're an experienced writer with a wide range of clips to your name, you may decide to specialize to work more efficiently. Freelancer Sam Greengard of West Linn, Oregon, wrote for a variety of national consumer magazines, writing about "pretty much anything and everything" until around the early 90s.

"At that point, I recognized that there was a pretty huge opportunity in business and technology writing, so I made a conscious effort to focus there," says Greengard. "I never told anyone that I wouldn't work for them. I simply stopped pitching editors in the general interest arena and began focusing on business and technology. It probably took about three to four years to really take off. Over the years, you conduct interviews, you read the trade magazines, you read material on the internet, and you develop a pretty strong body of knowledge," says Greengard. "By specializing, I don't have to go reinvent the wheel every time or research a topic I know nothing about. Chances are I know something about it, and I know enough to ask the right questions."

Kathy Sena of Manhattan Beach, California was a former technical writer and editor who freelanced on the side. In 1994, she started freelancing fulltime, and eventually developed specialties in health and lifestyle topics as well as parenting. She's found that specializing boosts her bottom line, and enhances her productivity.

"I write two self-syndicated health columns that are published in regional parenting and women's magazines in the U.S. and Canada. That has helped me break into other markets such as *Woman's Day* and *USA Today*," says Sena. "In addition to getting more assignments, I'm able to get higher rates because of specializing. Also, when you specialize, you tend to more-quickly build up a Rolodex full of great contacts — which leads to more article ideas and more work."

Finally, don't overlook the opportunity that specializing provides to let you explore topics that matter to you. Bob Bittner of Charlotte, Michigan created a niche for himself several years ago writing about animals, a long-term interest of his. "I wanted to break into *Family Circle* and I wanted to develop a specialty writing about animals and pets (yes, we have two cats)," says Bittner. "I had noticed that *Family Circle* ran a regular 'Pets' column, so I thought that was a good place to pitch, rather than trying to break in with an investigative health piece or a 'Women Who Make a Difference' story. Also, I figured that they'd get fewer well-targeted (and fresh) ideas for that section, so mine would really stand out. I must have done something right. My first pitch resulted in an assignment."

Since then, Bittner has branched out to cover nature/conservation topics as well as profiles. "For me, it's a matter of wanting to make a living writing about things that interest me. So, following those interests results in developing a variety of specialties," says Bittner. "I think one thread that I've found common in all of them is finding people who are passionate about what they do or passionate about some specific cause or interest ... I love being around people who are really excited about something, and I love finding these people and sharing them [with readers.]"

Will you create a specialty from the outset? Or will you choose a niche after a few years, once you've had a chance to write about a variety of topics? The choice is yours. Either way, by pitching yourself as a writer with a unique background and specialized knowledge, you'll boost your profile with editors and increase the likelihood that you'll be offered an assignment. And in today's marketplace, with so many writers competing for stories, that factor can only work to your advantage.

The All-Important Query: How to Make Yours Stand Out

"Where do you get your ideas, anyway?" I'm asked this question every time I teach. Students are surprised when I tell them that for me, the problem for me isn't coming up with ideas—there are millions of them floating around. The harder, time-consuming part is taking an idea, coming up with an interesting or newsworthy angle, tweaking it for a particular market, and proving that it's timely/interesting/important to the publication you're pitching.

When I started freelancing, I looked for—and found—ideas everywhere. But an idea by itself isn't enough. I had to decide what angle to take with the story and then select the markets that I thought would be most interested in the piece. I looked for story ideas that impacted my life or those of my friends, family members and neighbors. I also searched for local ideas that editors in New York or other cities might not have access to—this is a great way to get your foot in the door with a publication.

Tracking trends is another way to come up with ideas. For instance, simplifying and down-sizing your life, a growing trend in the 90s, continues to be big. Likewise, interest in complementary and alternative medicine remains strong, and should continue to be as the Baby Boomers age. Harnessing technology to save time at work or home is of ongoing interest. Since 9/11, we've become obsessed with security—at home, online, while traveling. And many topics are timeless, or "evergreen." Staying healthy. Becoming or staying financially secure. Finding and keeping a romantic partner. Raising smart, self-assured, healthy kids. Succeeding at your chosen career. Living a life that seems to have a purpose to it.

Take a look at your interests and background, and start developing a list of possible story ideas. If you're stuck, think about what's important to you and those around you. Study the markets you're interested in writing for to see what topics they cover, and the approach they take to different subjects. Look for ways to take a fresh look or a new spin on a tried-and-true subject, or for profiles or local events that magazine editors haven't come across.

The All-Important Query Letter

Once you have your idea, you'll have to write a query letter—this is how freelancers pitch editors. The importance of the query cannot be overstated, and it serves more than one purpose. A query is a letter of introduction. It's a sales pitch. It's your initial, and I think most important writing sample. It's also how you convince the editor to give you an assignment. Every query showcases your writing ability; it should also demonstrate your familiarity with the market itself and convince the editor that you are the perfect person to write the story.

There is no magic formula for writing queries, but most freelancers develop a rough template that they can use as a model for future letters. In chapter 1, I mentioned the basic four parts every query includes:

■ The lead to catch the editor's attention.
■ The "why write it" section to flesh out the idea and explain why it's a good fit for the publication.
■ The "nuts and bolts" paragraph which includes the technical aspects of the story such as word count, sources, format, and working title.
■ The "I-am-so-great" paragraph (or "ISG"), where you highlight your relevant qualifications, including your experience with the subject matter.

Here's the thing. I have to admit that when I started freelancing, I knew nothing about queries. My first queries were weak at best, atrocious at worst. I'd often begin them with snooze-inducing language "I'm a freelancer and I am writing you because I would like to write an article about…"

Think about it. When you read an article in a newspaper or magazine, the story doesn't start out by saying, "this will be an article on how reducing the fat in your diet can improve your health…" No, the article grabs your attention with a statistic, an interesting fact, a recent study, or an anecdote. Your query should open with the same kind of lead.

The second paragraph is where you prove your case to the editor and demonstrate why the story should be written. You might mention a time peg that explains the story's relevance if you didn't include that in your lead. You may include statistics or describe how this topic will impact readers' lives. How many people are affected by the subject you want to write about? How will readers benefit from this piece?

Remember, the editor wants to sell magazines, so you should be thinking the way she does. She's wondering whether this particular story will motivate someone standing in line at the grocery store or browsing through hundreds of periodicals at Borders or Barnes & Noble to pick up and purchase this particular issue of her magazine. You want to convince her that it will. (Many editors think of "cover lines" when they read queries—in other words, how would this piece be described in a short headline on the magazine's cover? You should be thinking the same way.)

The third paragraph, what I call the "nuts and bolts" paragraph, includes a brief outline of what the story will look like. I'll mention the angle, suggested word count, and possible sources like experts and "real people" I plan to interview. I'll also pitch related sidebars, boxes, or accompanying pieces like quizzes to round out the main story. I almost always include a working title and suggest an appropriate section of the magazine for the story if I can. (For example, "Are you interested in this topic for your 'Women's Health' department?") This makes it clear that I've read the magazine! Or I'll mention a recent story from the magazine to let the editor know I've looked at back issues. This certainly doesn't hurt; in fact it helps set your query apart from the dozens or even hundreds of queries she's wading through every month.

Finally, the fourth paragraph—the ISG. This is where I highlight my writing experience and any relevant background information to demonstrate that I'm "uniquely qualified" to write the article. If you're pitching a parenting story, mention that you're a stay-at-home mom of four children. Do you want to write about using the web for publicity? Include a sentence about your public relations background.

New writers often ask me if they should mention that they haven't been published yet. Well, the fact that you don't have clips (published copies of your work) may not be a reflection of your writing ability. In any case, you needn't advertise that fact in your query either. In other words, avoid language like, "Although I have never published anything…" or worse yet, "While I have been writing for years, no one seems to want to buy my work…" That's a definite turnoff. Instead, highlight the writing experience you do have and your unique qualifications. Include a brief overview of your general writing background (for example, writing for newsletters, newspapers, or local publications), and remember that your most important writing sample is the query itself.

While there is no magic formula to query-writing, your letter should capture the editor's interest, explain why readers will want to read the piece, describe how you plan to approach the subject, and convince the editor that you're the person for the assignment. Writing queries is a skill, and the more you do, the better you become at it. Consider these two actual queries (as with all the queries in this book, contact information for both writers and editors has been removed):

Dear Ms. Cook:

Most pregnant women are afraid that after the baby, their bodies will never be the same. They dread losing the fitness they have worked so hard to achieve but they don't want to risk their babies' health to keep up their workouts.

Most obstetricians agree that regular moderate exercise is beneficial to pregnant women as long as they were in good physical condition before pregnancy. However, mothers-to-be are advised to exercise at or below a certain heart rate to protect the baby's safety. Using a heart monitor allows these women to keep up their fitness program and reassures them that their child is safe.

I am interested in writing a short article for *Fitness* on the use of heart rate monitors while exercising by pregnant women. I will interview mothers who successfully employed monitors through pregnancy and several physicians for their recommendations on exercise during pregnancy. This piece will also remind readers of the value of using heart monitors for working out even if they are not pregnant or planning on becoming so.

I am a freelance writer interested in health and fitness issues and have enclosed two recent clips for your review. Please call me at your convenience to discuss this idea further.

Thank you for your time. I look forward to hearing from you soon.

Very truly yours,

Kelly K. James

Dear Megan:

A recent study published in The Lancet tracked a competitive runner who continued to train throughout her pregnancy. To ensure the safety of her babies (she delivered healthy twins), she wore a heart rate monitor to maintain a heart rate of 130-140 beats per minute.

Heart rate training is growing in popularity, not just for pregnant women, but for time-crunched exercisers seeking ways to work out more efficiently and safely. Using a heart rate monitor can make cardiovascular training more effective as it helps ensure that athletes work out as intensely (or as easily) as they are supposed to. Starting at $100, a heart rate monitor is an inexpensive investment that can be worth much more for women looking to improve their fitness.

Interested in a story about the use of heart rate monitors to train more efficiently? "Target Your Training: How a Heart Rate Monitor Can Make You Fitter" will give an overview of how these monitors can be used to maximize training. I'll include advice from athletic trainers and female athletes who use monitors regularly about how to get the most from a heart monitor; a possible sidebar might include a list of some of the different models available. Although I estimate about 800 words for this story, that's flexible depending on your needs.

Interested in this story for your "exercise.sports.fitness" section or as a short feature? As you know, I've written for Fit before as well as for other magazines including Cosmopolitan, Shape, Good Housekeeping, Modern Bride, and BRIDE'S.

I hope you'll find this story appropriate for a future issue of Fit; let me know if you have any questions about it. Thank you for your time; I look forward to hearing from you soon.

Very truly yours,

Kelly James-Enger

Both queries concern the same basic subject—using heart rate monitors. Yet the former was rejected (what I call "bonged") and the second was assigned. Why? While the first query isn't terrible, it isn't going to excite an editor, either.

First off, it's much too general. My lead starts out with an assumption that nearly anyone could make—that "most women" are afraid that pregnancy will irrevocably change their bodies. This is along the lines of saying something like "most parents want their children to grow up to be happy, well-adjusted adults" or "most of us want to live happy, fulfilling lives." Duh, right? Then in the second paragraph, I make the sweeping assertion that "most obstetricians" say that "moderate exercise" is beneficial as long as women keep their heart rate at or below a certain heart rate. How about some specifics here?

Second, it's inaccurate. If I would have done any background research, I would have discovered that the American College of Obstetricians and Gynecologists had recently rescinded its blanket recommendation that pregnant women exercise at or below 140 beats per minute. Instead, pregnant women are supposed to monitor their exertion levels and not push themselves too hard. If this editor knows anything about prenatal fitness, she'll catch this oversight immediately and know that I didn't spend any time researching my subject.

In addition to being, well, boring, I have misread the market. Think about it—how many women who read *Fitness* are pregnant or trying to become so? I'd guess 5 percent, probably fewer. Yet this query is directed at that tiny subgroup, although I do mention that the piece "will also remind readers of the value of using heart monitors for working out even if they are not pregnant or doing so." If I was pitching a magazine like *Fit Pregnancy*, this wouldn't be an issue. But I'm pitching a general women's fitness magazine.

And finally, my ISG, or "I-am-so-great," paragraph is actually not so great. Although I mention my interest in health and fitness, I don't do a very good job of convincing the editor of my qualifications to write the article, do I?

Now look at my "new and improved" query. Much better, isn't it? First off, my lead includes a double whammy—the mention of the recent study gives me both a time peg and evidence of a trend. *The Lancet* is a major British medical journal (along the lines of *The Journal of the American Medical Association* or *The New England Journal of Medicine*). I don't have to explain what it is because my editor works at a fitness magazine; otherwise, I'd include the phrase "a British medical journal."

In the second paragraph, I target the audience much more effectively.

While the study in question involved a pregnant woman, I immediately explain that heart rate monitors are growing in popularity, "not just for pregnant women, but for time-crunched exercisers seeking ways to work out more efficiently and safely." Aha! That's pretty much everyone who reads *Fit*, isn't it? (And is there anyone who wants to work out less efficiently and safely? Probably not.) Note that I also mention the benefits of using heart rate monitors and point out their affordability. At the time, a heart rate monitor only cost about $100—most readers would be able to purchase one. That's another selling point for this story.

Then, in the third paragraph, I've tried to make the editor's job easy. I've come up with a working title, which is a little long but gives an idea of what the piece will look like; I've told her the type of sources I plan to interview; and I've suggested an appropriate, service-oriented sidebar. I go on to estimate word count and then let her know that I've read the magazine by suggesting the department ("exercise.sports.fitness") the story seems right for. I also briefly mention my writing background; because I had worked with her before, I don't enclose clips.

But guess what? My ISG is still weak. Why? At the time, I'd been using a heart rate monitor during runs for several years—a fact that certainly makes me "uniquely qualified" to write about them. But it didn't occur to me to mention it in the query, even though I wound up using my experience as a first-person lead in the story itself. Moral of the story: nearly every query, now matter how good, can always be improved upon. And the more queries you write, the better they'll get.

But what about those first few queries you write? Here's the good news—even your first query can result in an assignment! In fact, I've seen dozens of new, inexperienced writers nail their first assignments with query letters we worked on in a magazine-writing class or workshop. Why did these letters succeed? Because the writers were pitching topics they had personal experience with.

Remember, none of these writers had published clips at the time they took a magazine-writing class, but they learned to analyze markets, develop compelling query ideas, and demonstrate why they were uniquely qualified to write for the markets. These successful first queries have included:

■ An emergency department administrator and former nurse whose first pitch was to an Illinois nursing magazine on a new law and how it would affect nurses practicing in the emergency department. Not only did her first query sell, she wound up writing another half-dozen articles for this publication. (Query by Alida Zamboni)

■ A stay-at-home mom's pitch about hidden backyard dangers. The query opened with an anecdote involving her three-year-old daughter, who had been rushed to the emergency room after eating mushrooms she discovered in the back yard. (Query by Jill Browning)

■ Another stay-at-home mom's pitch about local classes for about-to-be big brothers and sisters. (Query by Michelle Sussman)

■ A response to an ad seeking Chicago-area writers for a travel website that included the writer's knowledge of Chicago. (Letter by Tommy Newcomb)

■ A pitch to a trade magazine on more effective email techniques written by an IT consultant. (Query by Chris Bonney)

■ A query to a religious magazine about a new way to approach prayer written by a Christian who had discovered this method. (Query by Debbie Simler-Goff.)

■ A pitch to a major newspaper on how to eat healthfully at restaurants from a professional counselor and eating disorder specialist—who has also lost 70 pounds and kept it off. (Query by Susan Kutchin Pallant)

In the pages that follow, you'll find all of these queries; each is an excellent example of a strong ISG. Use these queries and the ones that follow throughout the book to make yours stand out from the pack.

Dear Ms. Boivin,

"Good Samaritan Hospital, this is Medic One calling for a channel assignment. We have a traumatic arrest."
"Medic One, go to Med Channel 8"
"OK, Good Sam, we were called to the scene of car vs tree and found a 32 y/o male patient who was entrapped...."

Every nurse working in an emergency department is not qualified to receive calls from prehospital care personnel. To do so, an ER nurse must be a certified ECRN (Emergency Communications Registered Nurse), which is mandated in the EMS Act of October 1997. The ECRN must be a quick thinker and able to make critical decisions under sometimes very stressful circumstances.

"ECRN: A Critical Component in the World of EMS" will inform your readers of the prerequisites for this position as well as the roles and responsibilities of an ECRN. This would be an excellent article to include in your "Nursing Roles" section. I plan to obtain quotes from EMS medical authorities across the state citing the importance of this nursing role.

Great timing for publication would be May as EMS personnel are honored during the third week of the month. Possible sidebars would include common abbreviations used in EMS, an explanation of the radio equipment used by an ECRN or a listing of the prerequisites to become an ECRN. One thousand to twelve hundred words would adequately cover the topic matter, but I could tighten or expand the article to meet your needs. I can provide photographs of a nurse at the telemetry radio or interacting with EMS personnel if desired.

As a part-time freelancer and an ECRN, I am qualified to submit an informative piece that can accurately describe this specialty area. I have been the Coordinator of a large EMS System for the last 15 years, and have educated hundreds of nurses who have attained ECRN certification. I am including a clip on an article I wrote for Domain, a national newsletter for NAEMSE (National Association of Emergency Medical Service Educators). Please call me if you have any questions regarding this query.

Thank you for your time. I look forward to your reply.

Sincerely,
Alida Zamboni, R.N., B.A.

Dear Ms. Schultz:

As a mother of three-year-old triplets who takes pride in keeping her kids safe indoors, I learned the hard way of the dangers lurking in our own backyard. My daughter ate a mushroom growing behind our sandbox, which resulted in an arduous overnight hospital stay filled with unpleasant treatments of activated charcoal. The severity of the moment was clear when the doctor told me matter-of-factly that she might need a kidney or liver transplant. Hours after the incident, the mushroom was deemed "nonpoisonous" by The Field Museum's team of biologists and my daughter was in the clear. Even so, the experience left me acutely aware of the fact that you don't mess with mushrooms.

Around 100 of the 10,000 different types of mushrooms are poisonous; wild mushrooms can grow anywhere and ingested in any amount they are considered dangerous. The American Association of Poison Control Centers (AAPCC) reports that in 2002, there were 8,722 cases of people ingesting wild mushrooms, with nearly 60 percent of these involving children ages five or under. Over 100,000 other children were exposed to toxic pesticides and plants in 2002, giving the phrase "wild outdoors" new meaning.

I'm sure other Chicago parents will want to know how they can protect their children from outdoor poison exposures. Would "Babyproof Your Backyard" be of interest to you for a ShortStuff piece? I'll interview poison emergency experts and AAPCC personnel and include information about poisonous mushrooms, plants and pesticides, what to do in case of ingestion and the new nationwide number to call for poison emergencies. Pulling from the AAPCC's new educational program that features Spike the porcupine as well as songs and activities, I will create useful sidebars to help put a parent's poison protection plan into immediate action.

Before becoming a freelance writer and stay-at-home mother, I worked in marketing communications, creating and writing for corporate web sites and newsletters. My work has been published in Gourmet and the industry newsletter Benefits and Compensation.

I hope you'll find this story appropriate for a future issue of Chicago Parent. I welcome your questions or advice. Thank you for your time and I look forward to hearing from you.

Sincerely,
Jill S. Browning

Dear Ms. Schultz,

All parents hear the sibling-related horror stories that come with a new baby:

"My daughter stopped potty training for six months when the new baby came."

"My son, a boy who would share any toy with any child, will not let his new little sister even come near his Bumble Ball."

"My daughter would not speak to me for days after we brought her new little brother home."

In Chicago Parent's August 2003 issue, David Jakubiak discussed preparing pets for the birth of a child. It stands to reason that parents would also want to prepare their children for a new baby, considering the difficulties with an older child that seem to follow. After all, there are multitudes of prenatal classes for parents, (even some for grandparents!) why not for the children in the family?

Are you interested in "Sibling Preparation Classes: Prenatal classes for the older sibling?" I'll include information on local hospitals such as Alexian Brothers Medical Center in Elk Grove Village and Edward Hospital in Naperville that offer such classes. I'll also include anecdotes from parents about their experiences.

I think an article of this nature would fit well into your Short Stuff section. I can write a piece of 200-500 words in length. As a mother who is considering having a second child, this is an issue that I believe must concern many parents in Chicagoland. I am also a published fiction writer, under my maiden name, Michelle Jensen, in magazines such as Writers' Journal and Romance and Beyond.

I hope you're interested in my article idea. If you have any questions, feel free to contact me by phone or email. I look forward to hearing from you!

Yours truly,

Michelle Sussman

Dear Diana:

I was excited to see your advertisement for non-fiction Chicago writers on craigslist. I'm seeking an opportunity just like this, and my background and your requirements are an excellent match. I've been consulting in Chicagoland since 1999, writing a multitude of various documents, like reports, technical speculations, and whitepapers for Fortune 500 companies. Consulting work has given me an opportunity to experience Chicago from many parts of the city. However, I am looking to expand my writing expertise beyond business and technical writing. This is why I believe I'd be perfect for this opportunity.

I love to travel and explore, visiting everything from the Chicago museums to the hidden garage-band bars near Boystown. For me, I like to try that new sushi restaurant on the corner, or see a local punk band in a Belmont bar, or get tickets to Mozart's requiem performed by the Chicago Symphony Orchestra. I have eclectic tastes, and I would be thrilled to write about them.

I also work with digital photography. I'll take my own digital photos and use Adobe Photoshop to improve their quality. I look forward to writing for NFT. I strive to meet and exceed expectations in my work. My resume is enclosed for your review.

Cheers,

Tommy Newcomb

Enclosure [he included a 200-word sample proposal per the ad]

Dear Mr. Skillman:

According to a March, 2005 report by Return Path, a leading e-mail marketing firm, one out of every five e-mails an association sends to its members is intercepted by the member's e-mail company as spam.

Internet Service Providers (ISPs) like Verizon, Netzero, and Comcast are taking action against spammers by filtering out e-mails that display the slightest characteristics of inappropriate content, ensuring they snare even the most clandestine spamming operations. This means that popular ISPs are dumping e-mails sent by associations exercising conscientious, permission-based messaging campaigns into the same spam bin as the most flagrant online pushers of Viagra. In some instances, an association's e-mail will be identified as spam for merely including "click here" too many times within the message area.

"Is Your Message Getting Through?" will be a 500-word article describing seven steps an association executive should take to avoid having their membership messages tagged as spam by commercial ISPs. I'll include practical tips such as minimizing the use of capital letters in the "Subject" line of an email, along with other simple, effective e-mail strategies. I'm proposing this piece for the "News & Know-How" section of Association Management.

I'm a freelance writer and former manager of IT Consulting at SmithBucklin Corporation. I am currently a consultant for small associations and have worked closely with technology clients, assisting them in their e-mail marketing efforts. My extensive experience and practical knowledge helping associations successfully overcome spam filters qualifies me to write this article, and I'm sure your readers will benefit from it.

Please consider "Is Your Message Getting Through?" for an upcoming issue of Association Management. Feel free to contact me at a convenient time; I'd be happy to discuss this piece in detail.

Sincerely,

Chris Bonney

Dear Ms. Bezek:

Jeremiah 17:9 says "The heart is deceitful above all things and desperately wicked: who can know it?" Despite this Biblical truth I found myself examining the "inner me" and often asked God to show me what my heart really looked like from His perspective.

God responded by teaching me Heart Drawing. Through Heart Drawing, the intercessor actually draws a heart image in his or her devotional notebook and then prayerfully considers areas of strengths and weaknesses as the Holy Spirit reveals them. These revelations are then illustrated on the heart image with varying colors and degrees of intensity to provide a "visual aid" to the intercessor of what's happening within them. As the intercessor grows and changes, so does their personal Heart Drawing.

Would your seasoned intercessor readers be interested in learning of a fresh approach for their introspective devotional time? "Heart Drawing: How to Draw Yourself Spiritually Fit" will give an overview of Heart Drawing. I'll include a first-person testimony along with a step-by-step guide of how to get started. A possible sidebar might include pictures of Heart Drawings with explanation. Although I estimate about 800 words for this story, that's flexible depending on your needs.

Interested in this story for your "Ideas" section or as a short feature? I'm a freelance writer who has experienced the joy and agony of prayer and has written for www.ninetyandnine.com, an evangelical webzine. Following are links to two of my articles for your review:

"The Holy Ghost is Watching You" www.ninetyandnine.com/archives/20000214/series.htm

"Little Talebearers" www.ninetyandnine.com/ar-chives/20000207series.htm

In Him,

Debbie Simler-Goff
Freelancer Writer

Dear Mr. Werland:

What a stormy, dark day! But spring has arrived to Chicago and although at times temperatures may still feel like winter, neighborhood restaurants are busily preparing outdoor seating. Chicagoans do not much mind draping themselves over a tablecloth to keep it in place while sitting under a heat lamp as wind whips around their table just to enjoy an outdoor meal! We just adore going to restaurants, and we love eating outdoors, especially after surviving endless freezing, dreary months.

When trying to lose weight, meals outside our home can be a challenge. Whether eating out for business, pleasure, in our hometown or away, we can enjoy dining out and still lose unwanted pounds. And warm weather offers extra opportunities to burn calories!

Q has become my new favorite Sunday Section, for advice, fun and the education it provides. My article, 10 Tips to Lose Weight While Eating Out this Summer, will offer practical solutions to the age-old problem of sticking to a weight loss plan while eating away from home. In 2002, Arlene Schusteff interviewed me for a "Smart Talk" piece she wrote on avoiding fast-food traps, however, this piece would be more specific to summer eating.

I am a Licensed Professional Counselor and Eating Disorder Specialist. I lead weight loss and stress management workshops in Chicagoland and South Florida. I work with clients of all ages and help them develop healthy eating and thinking habits for life and ways to manage stress without turning to food. Having maintained an over 70-pound weight loss for 12 years, while dining out probably a bit too often, I teach the strategies that work!

I have contributed several pieces to "Q Diary." In addition, I have written several articles for Today's Chicago Woman that focus on weight loss and stress management. I would be happy to send you clips if you wish.

Please let me know if there are questions I can answer for you and I look forward to hearing from you.

Susan Kutchin Pallant

Make Your Queries More Effective

All right. Now that you've seen some excellent examples of powerful ISGs, let's address a few other query concerns. You'll make your queries more effective if you keep these tips in mind:

Choose your (delivery) weapon. Should you send your queries via snail mail or email? When I started freelancing fulltime almost 10 years ago, all my queries were sent via snail mail. Today, I'm more likely to send them by email instead. If you're worked with an editor before, if you know the editor prefers email queries, or the guidelines tell you to email, then email your queries. If none of the above apply, choose snail mail. (Believe it or not, there are plenty of editors out there who still prefer snail mail!)

If you do email a query, use the subject line of your email message to catch the editor's attention and give her a preview of your email contents. If you're querying a magazine editor, you write something like "connection between stress and belly fat" in the subject. If you know the editor, include your name—"query from Kelly James-Enger." If you've been referred to the person, you may want to mention the person's name in the subject header.

When emailing, don't include attachments. Unless your editor has specifically requested an attachment. (By the way, always ask if he or she prefers an attachment or to simply include the story itself in the body of the email.) Most editors and agents won't open attachments from writers unknown to them—they can carry viruses that can corrupt your PC, even your Mac. If you do include an attachment, ask the editor what program she'd like it saved in—for example, using a .doc extension is a word document, .txt signifies a text-only format. The same goes for graphic attachments or photos—does your editor prefer a jpeg or a tif?

Employ the "24-hour rule." As a new freelancer, I used this rule to keep me focused. Simply stated, within 24 hours of receiving a rejection (what I call a "bong") from an editor, two things would happen. First, I'd resubmit the query to another market. That got my query letter out there for another potential sale. Second, I'd send a new query to the editor who had rejected me, starting with language like, "Thank you very much for your response [not rejection!] to my query about the connection between stress and belly fat. While I'm sorry you can't use the idea at this time, I have another for you to consider." Then I'd include my new query. The 24-hour rule enabled me to turn each rejection into two new opportunities. Just as important, it kept my name in front of editors I was pitching. And getting back in touch with editors immediately helped me build relationships even before I'd written for their publications. Finally, it also eliminated the question of "what should I do now?" that I would have otherwise wondered about after receiving a bong. I didn't get derailed by the rejection; I simply used it as opportunity to apply my 24-hour rule. (Is the 24-hour rule too ambitious for you? Then how about a 48-hour rule? A three-day rule? A one-week rule? Choose the timeframe that works for you and your schedule, and start looking at those dreaded bongs as opportunities rather than rejections— and a way to create a relationship with an editor that will lead to your first assignment.)

Tricks of the Trade: Nonfiction Marketing and Research Techniques

Whether you write about a variety of subjects or specialize in just a few areas, the basics of freelancing still apply. To be a successful nonfiction writer, in addition to developing compelling story ideas, finding markets for your work, and pitching ideas to editors, you have to be able to conduct research, find and interview experts and other sources, and write accurately and well. Oh yeah, and you have to make your deadlines, deliver what you promised, and basically make your editors' and clients' jobs easier.

Gather Your Facts: Researching and Writing the Article

One of the benefits of writing about subjects you already have a background in is that you don't have to start from scratch. Still, though, you'll need to do some research, whether it's locating or double-checking statistics, tracking down medical journal articles, or interviewing sources. The best tip I can give you for research? Become friends with the reference librarians at your local library. They can be invaluable when you're having trouble tracking down a specific piece of information or an obscure study.

When you're researching, don't be afraid to call on resources, associations, governmental agencies and organizations related to your topic. Call or email and ask for the media affairs person—he or she may be a font of information. In the chapters that follow, you'll find hundreds of helpful resources that will help you find the information you need—or the people who can help you locate it.

What about your human sources? How do you find experts? What do you say when you contact them? And how do you actually conduct an interview? Interviewing often strikes fear into the heart of new freelancers, but follow this simple game plan and you'll locate the right experts for your articles, make the most of your time with them, and obtain compelling quotes to make your stories stand out.

Step 1: Locate Your Sources

First off, you have to decide who you'll interview for the story. Perhaps your background research has uncovered potential sources in other newspaper, magazine, or medical journal articles. In other cases, you'll start from scratch. There are a number of efficient ways to find qualified experts, and the methods you use may depend on the topic and nature of the expertise you seek.

The Encyclopedia of Associations

Today, it's easy to use google.com or another online search engine to hunt for potential sources. But let's start with an old-fashioned method that works. Check out the monster three-volume Encyclopedia of Associations, which will be found on reserve at your local library. The encyclopedia includes more than 20,000 U.S.-based organizations that cover everything from medicine to gardening to hobbies to sports to charity groups.

Use the index to locate the appropriate subject, and read through the descriptions of the organizations listed to find one that meets your needs. (When there are several to choose from, I usually start with the largest or most well-established.) Then call the association (calling usually provides a quicker turn-around than emailing), and ask for the media affairs or public relations department. Once you've connected with that person, explain that you're a freelancer working on a story on fill-in-the-blank and would like his or her help hooking you up with a member of the organization who can help you.

The organization's PR person can suggest appropriate members, and may often offer people you would not have thought of otherwise. You can be as specific as you like with your request—say, "I'm looking for a nutritionist who works with middle-aged Hispanic-American women to help them reduce their risk of diabetes," instead of "I need to ask a nutritionist about diabetes prevention strategies." If you prefer an expert with certain qualifications, like affiliation with a major university or significant media experience, tell the PR person. He'll be able to provide you with names and contact information of experts who will fit the bill.

Colleges and Universities

Depending on the type of story you're doing, you may consider calling on a college or university as well. For a local piece, you may be fine with a professor at the state school; for national stories, I tend to stick with major, well-known universities. I'm based in Chicago, so I tend to use Midwestern-based schools—I figure NYU and UCLA already get lots of play. With schools, I take the same approach I would with an organization; I call and speak with the public affairs or media relations department and ask for referrals to an appropriate faculty member to interview.

Book Authors

Another easy way to find an expert for a story is to look for a book on the subject—preferably a recent one. Book authors actually seek out publicity—the more often they're interviewed, the more frequently their books are mentioned. Check out your local bookstore, and either track down the author through a search engine or call the publisher and ask for the public relations department. Someone there will be happy to hook you up with the author for an interview.

Online Resources

There are also several online resources you can use to locate experts. The most popular is media.prnewswire.com, often called "Profnet." You have to be a published writer to register to use the service (the online form asks what publications you've written for), but it's free and relatively easy to use. You can search an extensive database of experts or submit a query specifying what you're looking for ("a certified public accountant who's also the mother of triplets") that's sent to PR agencies, universities, corporations, hospitals, and experts. You can choose what types of institutions your query is sent to, and how you'd like to receive responses—i.e., via phone or email.

In addition to Profnet, there are a variety of other online resources available to help you locate sources including:

■ www.mediaresource.org – Includes science and technology experts.
■ www.experts.com – Includes experts in a variety of fields.
■ experts.mediamap.com – Similar to Profnet; includes thousands of experts.
■ www.facsnet.org/tools – Includes experts in three areas: business/economics, science and technology, and environment and land use.

Step 2: Hook Up

Once you've determined who you want to interview, it's time to make contact. Sure, it's nerve-wracking at first, but keep in mind that just about everyone finds it flattering to be asked about a subject they know lots about. In most cases, I call and introduce myself, and then explain why I'm calling. If I've been referred by an organization, PR person, or online resource, I mention that as well.

Tell the expert the nature of the story you're writing, the reason why you're contacting her, how much time the interview will take, and what you want to ask her about. Note that I don't conduct the interview during that first call, preferring to give the expert some time to prepare for our actual interview even if it occurs later that same day.

In some cases, you may prefer to send an email to make initial contact. Here's a brief script you can adapt to your own purposes:

Dear Ms. Smith:

I'm a freelance writer working on a story on the benefits of using a life coach to improve your fitness program for Experience Life magazine [introduce yourself/explain the nature of your story and the market]. My editor gave me your name, and I think you'd make an excellent resource for the story [explain how/why you're contacting her person]. Are you available for a brief (10-15 minute) telephone interview in the next couple of days? [Tell the expert what to expect and what your deadline is]. I'm happy to work around your schedule and look forward to hearing back from you soon.

Thanks very much,
Professional Writer

Note that I almost always conduct interviews by telephone rather than email. Phone interviews are more immediate, less time-consuming, and put the burden on the writer to transcribe the answers rather than requiring an expert to type them out. However, in rare cases (usually when the expert specifically requests it), I will do an interview via email. Keep in mind that the answers may sound more "canned" than they would with a phone or in-person interview.

Step 3: Conduct the Interview

After you confirm the time and date of your call, take the time to do some background research on the subject you're interviewing the expert about. Don't expect the expert to spoon-feed you basic info you can easily locate ahead of time. If you're new to interviews, you may also want to write out an outline of the questions to cover. Remember to include basics such as:

■ Name, job title, and academic degrees, if applicable
■ Contact information (snail mail address, email, landline, cell phone, fax)
■ Book title(s), if applicable
■ Age and other personal information, if applicable. (For example, if you're interviewing parents for a story, you may want to ask for the names and ages of their children.)

Once you've prepared for the interview, make the call, and make sure to ask, "is this still a good time for you talk?" after you get the pleasantries out of the way. That sets a positive tone for the interview and shows that you appreciate the person's time. At least one time in four, a source will ask if I can call back in a few minutes, or later that day.

If you want to record the interview, ask permission of the source—in some states, it's illegal to tape someone without consent. Otherwise, you can transcribe or jot notes as you go along.

After you get the basics out of the way, proceed with your interview questions. Try to ask open-ended rather than closed-ended questions for better quotes—for example, instead of asking, "Professor, are today's children more likely to be involved in a school shooting now than they were 10 years ago?," ask, "Professor, are school shootings on the rise, and if so, can you tell me the reasons why?"

After you've finished asking your questions, be sure to give the expert a "softball" at the end, like "Is there anything about this subject you'd like to add, or something you think readers should know?" I often get the juiciest quotes from that last question. Close the interview by thanking the expert and telling him or her that you'll be in touch with any follow-up questions.

Finally, I send a personal note thanking the expert for the interview and saying that I'll be in touch when the story runs. Each only takes me a minute or two, and it helps me develop an excellent network of experts for future stories. That cuts my research time the next time I write another story on a similar subject—or just need an expert in that subject area again.

A Case Study:
Tracking an Article from Start to Finish

Non-writers often don't understand the amount of time and work that goes into an article, even (or especially!) shorter pieces. The time span between the initial query to publication of the article can easily last six or nine months, often longer. And this assumes a fairly speedy reply to the query—my record is an incredible 26 months lapsing between mailing the query and getting the phone call to assign the story. During that time, I'd married, changed my name, and changed careers…fortunately, I was still living at the same address or I don't think she would have tracked me down!

If you're a new writer, you may also wonder about the article-writing process. What do you do first? How much time should you expect to spend researching and writing your first story? In general, a freelance magazine article is going to involve the following steps:

1) Pitch an idea via a query letter, which is assigned by an editor. (This step is omitted if the editor contacts you with a story he came up with.)

2) Do additional background research (if necessary—you may have done this already to write your query) to identify possible experts, sources, and other sources of information for the piece.

3) Contact and interview sources, and conduct other research such as locating relevant statistics or obtaining copies of journal articles.

4) Write the initial draft of your article.

5) Edit, finish, and turn in the article.

6) Perform any necessary revisions as requested by your editor.

7) Get paid—and get published.

However, the process isn't always so simple. If you're a new free-lancer, let's walk through the process with one of my first fitness pieces to give you an idea of what you can expect. I queried *Shape* about an article about relocating with a fitness perspective (see the next page). Having heard nothing, I sent a follow-up letter a few months later (see the following page); but took eight months from my original query to hear from the editor. Little did I know when I pitched the idea that it would be 19 months before I saw the finished article in print.

Dear Ms. Moline:

When Abby moved from Atlanta to Minneapolis, she was in for a shock. Living in the south, she had enjoyed bicycling, hiking and rock climbing all year long. Minneapolis meant bitterly cold winters where outdoor exercise was out of the question, and after a few months, she found herself feeling out of shape and depressed. It didn't help that she didn't know anyone in town except the people she worked with.

One year later, Abby's back in the fitness swing. She still hikes and bikes during the summer months and has learned to roller-blade. In the winter, she stays in shape with exercise videos and indoor roller-blading. She's also in a basketball league, and this winter is taking tap dance lessons. While she isn't crazy about the -50° wind chill, she enjoys the indoor sports and has made a lot of new friends from them, too.

Although the readers of Shape make their health and fitness a priority, moving to a new city, a new state, or even just across town often disrupts a woman's exercise routine—but it can also be the opportunity to break out of a fitness rut.

I am interested in writing a short article for your magazine on how to survive a move to a new place. The piece will include anecdotes such as the above and will include advice on how to make the transition easier. This short, helpful article might appear in "Rut Buster" or "Inner Shape" or could be run as a short feature. As a freelance writer (who has survived four moves in four years) and exercise buff, I believe I can bring a unique perspective to this topic. I am familiar with the tone and format of your magazine and have enclosed two recent clips for your review.

Thank you for your time. I look forward to hearing from you soon.

Very truly yours,

Kelly K. James

Dear Ms. Moline:

I write to follow up on my query about moving which I submitted to you in March. Since I haven't had a response from you yet, I've taken the liberty of enclosing a copy of that letter for your convenience.

If you have any questions, please give me a call. If I don't hear from you in another six weeks or so, I'll assume you can't use this idea at the moment and may market it elsewhere.

Thank you for your time and consideration. I look forward to hearing from you soon.

Very truly yours,

Kelly James-Enger

Here's a look at the specific steps taken—and the time involved—to write a seemingly straightforward 600-word fitness story:

1. Come up with the Idea

This was an easy one. I'd moved several times in the previous years. For me, part of the fun of living in a new city was finding running routes and exploring my new home on foot. When one of my friends relocated from sunny Atlanta back to the Twin Cities, I had the perfect lead for my query...which I used.

2. Find an Appropriate Market

As usual, I started with *Writers Market*, looking at the guidelines for women's fitness magazines. *Shape, Fitness, Fit* and *Self* all seemed like possibilities, but *Shape* had a column called "Rut Buster" that I thought the idea was perfect for...so I pitched the story there first.

3. Write the Query

The query didn't take me too long to write. It's an okay query but not spectacular—I could have done a better job of fleshing out the idea.

My ISG paragraph is pretty good though—who better to write this piece than me?

4. Follow up

I didn't hear from the editor, so I sent a follow-up letter in June, asking if she was interested in the story idea. (By the way, six weeks is a long time to wait when you send a follow-up letter—today, I'd ask for a response within two weeks.)

5. Phone Call/Assignment

In November, Suzanne Schlossberg, an editor at *Shape*, called to assign the piece. We discussed the length (600 words), the pay ($1.20/word for all rights), the deadline, and possible sources for the piece. (Note: now that I am further along in my career, I usually don't sign "all-rights" contracts because they prevent me from selling any reprint rights to the story in the future. But as a new freelancer, I was more concerned with amassing clips and less concerned with the rights I was giving up.)

Suzanne wanted me to interview a sports psychologist as well as a ski instructor, who could comment on what to do—and not do—when you took up a new sport. She had a pretty clear idea of what she wanted out of the story. Because I was a relatively new writer, she also asked me to write an outline of the piece before I started. (She also could have conceivably asked me to write "on spec," or on speculation. When you write on spec, you don't have a formal assignment, but the editor offers to read the finished piece—and possibly purchase it.)

6. Find my Sources

The next step was to find appropriate sources for the story. My friend Abby was my first call. I gave her a buzz and told her I'd be interviewing her for the story. I then called the American Running and Fitness Association and asked the public affairs person to suggest a qualified sports psychologist to interview. She recommended Jack Lesyk, Ph.D., director of the Ohio Center for Sport Psychology. To locate a ski instructor, I simply put in the words "Jackson Hole ski instruction" into a search engine (today, I'd use www.google.com) and found a number of ski schools. I called one and asked for an extroverted, experienced instructor, and was given Jamie Mackintosh's name and number. I called all of my sources and lined up the interviews.

7. Draft Rough Outline

Per Suzanne's request, I wrote an outline of the piece and emailed it to her for her approval; she said it looked fine. While submitting an outline does take additional time, it ensures that you and your editor are on the same page as far as the story goes.

8. Prepare for/Conduct Interviews

Using my outline as a guide, I made a short list of questions to ask my sources. I conducted all three interviews by phone and then transcribed my notes. I also sent personal thank-yous to Abby, Jack, and Jamie, and told them I'd be in touch with any follow-up questions or to let them know when the story was published.

9. Write First Draft

After reading through my interview notes, I wrote my first draft. I used a first-person lead, at Suzanne's suggestion. (During our phone conversations, I'd mentioned that when I moved to St. Louis, I also signed up for a marathon training group and ran my first marathon. She thought this was a great way to start the story. Well, duh. Why didn't I think of that when I was writing the query?)

10. Edit/Finalize Draft

Not surprisingly, my original draft was too long—I then went back through the piece and pared it down to close to 600 words. (My rule of thumb is to be within 10 percent of the word count, but I try to get as close to the exact word count as possible.) I set it aside for a day or so and then came back to finish the final draft—reading through it word by word until I was satisfied that it was perfect, or at least as close as I would get. I turned it in to Suzanne the day before deadline, in December 1997. (Oh, by the way—turn in stories a day or two early and editors will remember you. Why? Because most writers turn in their work the day it's due—or later.)

11. Phone Call From Suzanne re Story

Suzanne said I had a great start to the story, but had some edit requests. She wanted me to tighten the lead and to get stronger quotes from Jack and Abby. I made notes of her suggestions and we agreed to a deadline for the revision.

12. Revise Story

I called Jack and Abby back, obtained additional quotes and revised the story per Suzanne's suggestions. Turned in the piece in January 1998, and then waited...

13. Good News!

Suzanne called to tell me the piece had been accepted. She asked me to turn in my fact-checking material (in this case, the names and telephone numbers of everyone I interviewed) and said that she was "putting payment through"—meaning I would see my check soon. (Some magazines want you to provide them with an invoice while others don't use them. Don't forget to ask your editor whether you need to send one.)

14. Get Paid!

Woo hoo! The check arrived sometime in February…and I happily cashed it. Then I waited to see the piece in print.

15. Get Published!

Alas, the story didn't run in June as originally thought, but finally appeared in the October 1998 issue. I called my sources to let them know the date of the issue and the page the story started on, leaving my phone number in case they had questions. A full 19 months after my initial query, I saw the bylined article in the magazine.

On the pages that follow, you'll find my original story, and the revised version. I think Suzanne's suggestions made for a stronger piece—that's the benefit of working with a good editor. While some writers tend to be protective (sometimes overly protective, in my opinion) of their words, I'm usually not that sensitive if an editor wants to tweak a lead or reorganize a piece—it often makes the story better.

However, there have been several occasions when I turned in a story only to have it so badly mangled that I barely recognized it when it ran. Was I happy about it? No, but when it comes to a standoff between you and the editor, your editor will nearly always win. Choose your battles, and never let an argument over your story become personal.

Kelly James-Enger
1312 DuPont Avenue #D
Morris, IL 60450
(815) 942-8521
kjames@matrix.uti.com

617 words
Rights per written contract

Get a Move On:
Relocating Can Jump-Start Your Fitness Routine
By
Kelly James-Enger

When I was 25, I graduated from law school and moved to St. Louis from a small town for my first "real" job. I was miserable the first couple of months—I'd never lived in a large city before, I knew only two people in town, and going from the laid-back lifestyle of a student to 60-hour workweeks was a shock. The only constant in my life was my running—my morning runs helped me get to know my neighborhood and cope with the pressures of my new career. I even found that living in a big city had advantages—I joined a marathon-training program that revitalized my training and helped me successfully complete my first marathon that fall. Participating in the program also helped me meet dozens of other local runners at our Sunday morning runs and eventually make friends in my new location.

Relocating—whether it's across town or across the country—is often the perfect time to reevaluate your exercise program. "Relocating can be an opportunity to breathe some new life into your fitness routine," says Jack J. Lesyk, sports psychologist and Director of the Ohio Center for Sport Psychology in Beachwood, Ohio. Lesyk suggests looking at your current workout program and asking yourself what you really enjoy and whether you'd benefit from a change. "Maybe you've gotten a little tired of doing indoor machine workouts and you can now try some different outdoor activities," he says.

Moving from one climate to another may force you to change your exercise strategy. My friend Abby biked, hiked, and rock-climbed year-round when she lived in Atlanta, but now lives in Minneapolis. Although she still bikes during the summer, she's found creative ways to maintain her fitness during the cold Minnesotan winters—she rollerblades indoors, plays basketball at the Y, and takes tap and ballet classes.

No matter how busy you are during those first few months in a new place, make time for working out. "Exercising can help you maintain a 'centeredness' when other things are changing," says Leysk. "Moving involves a lot of stress and changes, so you want to hang on to something familiar and comforting. It helps psychologically, not just physically."

Keeping fit can also help you break into your new community and meet new people who have similar interests. If you worked out at a gym before, make finding one a priority—and try to go at the same time of day so you'll begin to recognize people. Check the yellow pages for "health clubs" to see what your new city offers and if they have a running or biking club you can join—I've found this is another way to make friends right away.

If your move inspires you to try a new sport, make sure you know what you're doing before you start. "Taking lessons with a professional instructor will help you learn correct technique and progress much more quickly than if you try to learn on your own," says Jamie Mackintosh, a professional ski instructor and training coordinator at the Jackson Hole Ski School in Wyoming. Although being in good physical shape will help you master new sports, Mackintosh adds "when you try something new, it's normal to be sore no matter how fit you are. Your body is adjusting to using the muscles in a different pattern."

Even the most well-organized move can disrupt your regular routine, but staying fit will help you handle the stress and make your transition less difficult. I should know—I've moved five times in the past six years, and running has helped me survive every one. Even better, it helps a new place feel more like home, no matter where I live.

-30-

A Case Study

Kelly James-Enger
1312 DuPont Avenue #D
Morris, IL 60450
(815) 942-8521
kjames@matrix.uti.com

625 words
Rights per contract

Get a Move On:
Jump-Start Your Fitness Routine When You Relocate
by
Kelly James-Enger

When I was 25, I made the biggest move of my life—from a small college town to St. Louis for my first job as a lawyer. I'd never lived in a big city before, I was working sixty hours a week, and I was lonely. When I heard about a marathon-training program that fall, I figured it would be a good way to meet people—and I'd always dreamt of running a marathon.

For the next three months, I spent Thursday evenings listening to different experts give advice on training, nutrition, and stretching and Sunday mornings doing long runs with fellow program participants. By the end of November, I was in the best shape of my life—and completed my first marathon in 4:11.

Relocating—whether across town or across the country—is the perfect time to add something different to your exercise mix. "Relocating can be an opportunity to breathe some new life into your fitness routine," agrees Jack Lesyk, sports psychologist and Director of the Ohio Center for Sport Psychology in Beachwood, Ohio. Why not try a high-energy spinning class instead of step aerobics? Yoga may be the perfect antidote to a weightlifting program that's become a bore, and experimenting with new machines like the popular elliptical trainers can bring back the excitement to your workouts.

Your move may even force you to change your routine. When my friend Abby lived in Atlanta, she biked, hiked, and played tennis and basketball year-round—until her company transferred her to Minneapolis.

"I dreaded the Minnesota winters because I love to exercise outside," she says. "But some days it's 20 below here. You're not even supposed to be outside!" Still, she admits, Minneapolis has its perks. "I had always wanted to learn to roller-blade, but Atlanta was too hilly. Now I roller-blade outdoors in the summer and at the Metrodome in the winter." She adds, "And I've taken tap and ballet classes, too—I'd never have done that before."

Trying something new can also motivate you to work out during this busy time. "Exercising can help you maintain a 'centeredness' when other things are changing," says Leysk. "Moving involves a lot of stress and changes, so you want to hang on to something familiar and comforting. It helps psychologically, not just physically."

If you're inspired to try a new sport, consider some initial instruction. "Taking lessons with a professional instructor will help you learn correct technique and progress much more quickly than if you try to learn on your own," says Jamie Mackintosh, a professional ski instructor and training coordinator at the Jackson Hole Ski School in Wyoming. And cut yourself some slack—even if you're an expert in one sport, it takes time to master a new one. "When you try something new, it's normal to be sore no matter how fit you are," says Mackintosh. "Your body is adjusting to using the muscles in a different pattern."

When you move to a new place, scope out what your community offers. Stop by the local bike or running store to ask about clubs and races, and check out area health clubs. (Look for a gym that offers a wide range of equipment and classes so you'll have plenty of options to choose from.) Community centers, park districts and recreation departments, and community colleges are also good places to inquire about fitness classes and activities.

Finally, don't forget that relocating is an adventure. I've moved four times in five years, and each move has boosted my training, encouraging me to set new goals with the promise of undiscovered running trails and a sense of starting over. A new home signals the beginning of a new chapter in your life. Make this one your best yet.

-30-

Section Two: The Top 10 Hottest Specialties

An Apple a Day: Writing About Health

You want to write about health? Good idea. Nearly every periodical runs health-related stories, and for good reason—this topic affects us all regardless of sex, race, age, income or profession. Parents want to know how to treat and prevent childhood diseases and ensure their kids' well-being. Women read up on gynecological issues like premenstrual syndrome, pregnancy and birth, and how to avoid diseases like breast and ovarian cancer. Baby boomers seek ways to lower their risk of disease and improve the quality of their lives.

Whether it's a newsy article on the latest developments in AIDS research, a straightforward piece on how to reduce your risk of heart disease, or a rundown of alternative therapies like magnets, aromatherapy and herbal remedies, health writing is a continually growing and lucrative field. While it doesn't hurt to have a medical background to specialize in this area, the key to succeeding is being able to conduct accurate research. You must know where to locate information and be able to separate fact from fiction, speculation from science. You may also have to translate complicated medical concepts and jargon into language that readers can comprehend, and if appropriate, apply to their lives.

Because of this, it can be challenging to break into the health-writing field. I suggest you look for topics you're uniquely qualified to write about, but keep in mind that your experience is not enough. In other words, simply because you have diabetes doesn't mean you can sell a 1,500-word feature on the disease to a men's magazine with your first query. While your personal experience described in your ISG will certainly help you get an assignment, look for ways to go beyond your personal story and make the topic of interest to the editor you're pitching.

Let's say you have diabetes, and want to break into the health-writing field. Think about the challenges you've faced, and how to spin them into possible stories. If you're a new writer, you'll likely have the most success with short pieces while you garner clips and writing experience. You may automatically think about specialty magazines that cover diabetes as possible markets, but don't stop there. Depending on your background and experience, you might pitch the following:

■ A piece for your local paper featuring travel tips, tying in the new restrictions on carry-on baggage (your ISG mentions how you've recently traveled with your insulin medication and needles)

■ A story on how the glycemic index works, and what types of foods are "low GI" versus "high GI" (your ISG explains that as a diabetic, you're familiar with the GI and base your meals around low GI foods)

■ A story on the rising incidence of type II diabetes among children, and what can be done to combat it (your ISG mentions your experience with diabetes)

■ A business story on how more companies are offering meal-replacement bars and shakes designed to help people control their blood sugar (in your ISG, you say that you've tried a variety of them)

■ A story on effective ways to quit smoking (in your ISG, you share your personal experience of how you quit when your doctor warned you smoking is especially dangerous for diabetics.)

And that's just a start! From covering diabetes-related topics, you can easily branch out into other health topics, including medicine, nutrition, fitness, and wellness. Start with what you know and grow from there.

The Nuts and Bolts: How to Write about Health

Accuracy is Paramount
While editors and markets vary in terms of their approaches to health stories, there are a number of basic strategies to keep in mind when writing about this subject. The first and most important is the need to be both accurate and clear. Whether you're recommending that readers take a certain amount of vitamin C to reduce the risk of contracting a cold or describing how to perform a monthly breast exam, you must be able to write with specificity while avoiding medical jargon

or terms that the average reader won't understand.

Of course if you're writing for a more specialized audience such as a professional medical journal or a trade magazine aimed at physicians, this may be less of a concern. Many health writers have developed a background in their subject areas, but readers probably don't have the same level of expertise. When writing for a general audience, you may have to explain some basic concepts—when in doubt, let the market and your editor be your guides. If you're writing about heart disease for a men's magazine, the first time you use the word "arteriosclerosis," for example, you should explain that it's commonly known as "hardening of the arteries," and refers to a variety of conditions that cause artery walls to thicken and lose elasticity. A medical audience, on the other hand, likely won't need this explanation.

Be Timely

Much of health-based reporting is founded on newly published studies and the latest research. Health journalists must stay on top of breaking news and be able to pitch ideas that tie into the latest headlines; try to have a news peg in your health-related queries to convince the editor of the story's timeliness. For example, when the Body Mass Index ("BMI") was first introduced as the new standard of healthy weights in June 1998, dozens of articles were immediately published explaining what it was and how to calculate your own. Other articles questioned its usefulness and how this new standard would affect health care.

Has a new drug recently become available? Is a new fad diet sweeping the country? Has a new study recently questioned a traditionally-held medical belief? Find something timely about the story you're pitching and highlight it in your query. This will demonstrate your familiarity with this subject area and help you break in with new markets as well.

Even if you're pitching an evergreen topic, look for a way to make the story timely—in other words, to answer the question, "why write about this topic now?" If you can't answer that question, you may want to look for another topic to pitch.

Get a Handle on Research

With hundreds of thousands of research articles published every year, there is no shortage of studies that can be tweaked into queries, cited in articles, or used to support your writing. Yet not all studies are created equal. In general, the larger the study, the better. Research on humans is given more weight, and may be more credible than studies conducted on rats, mice or other animals. Most magazines will expect you to turn in copies of any research articles you refer to for fact-checking by them, so you can't fudge here. Make sure that you understand how the research was conducted—was it a controlled, clinical trial, for example, or simply a review article summarizing the published research—before you cite the results in a story.

Some factors to keep in mind when reviewing research studies include:

Was the study randomized and double-blind (meaning that the researchers themselves were unaware of which subjects comprised the control group and which were the experimental)? Was it a controlled study, meaning that the researchers sought to change only one variable out of many?

How many people were involved and over what period of time? Usually, the greater the number of subjects involved and the longer a study period lasts, the more weight it carries.

What were the demographics of the people involved? Were both men and women included? What ages were they? How were they selected to participate in the study?

Was it an animal or human study? The results of an animal study can suggest what may happen in humans, but usually isn't considered conclusive.

Was the study conducted by a major university or hospital? Was it an independent study or was it underwritten in whole or in part by a corporation or association that may have a vested interest in the results of the research (for example, a bottled-water supplier supporting a study on how much water is needed for optimal health)?

Did the results confirm or agree with existing research or were the results surprising? Why?

Does the study have significant health implications or consequences for people? If so, for whom?

When writing about health, you simply can't take research at face value. Be leery about trumpeting its significance, says Margaret Littman, a freelancer based in Chicago who specializes in health and business topics. "You have to be critical of any studies you read and any medical information you get. I find editors want someone who can question a doctor, question a medical expert, and question a study finding," says Littman. "Also, you definitely have to know the terminology, like was it a double-blind study or a study that was done on rats or on humans. In health writing, there are so many cases where there is a small study and it gets blown out of proportion and misreported as something that can apply to humans or apply in some ways that haven't been proven yet."

Consider the Audience

Writers should keep in mind that the majority of health writing is service-oriented. Why is someone reading this story? What will she gain by taking the time to finish it? How will it affect her life? While medical information can be dry, good health writers find a way to impart it in an entertaining or new way. "You can't just quote the experts…you need to find some way to get readers to relate to the information, whether it's anecdotes or humor," says Littman. "Just because these are serious topics doesn't mean you have to be grave all the time. I don't think you can be, if you expect anyone to read things."

And while some topics are evergreen (that's why a time peg is so important!), successful health writers come up with new ways to pitch tried-and-true stories. "To a certain extent in health writing, more than in other categories, you can repeat the obvious," says Littman. "People know that the way to lose weight is to exercise more and eat less, and people know the way not to get sick is to wash their hands, but there are no magic formulas. A lot of it is repeating the sensible advice whenever you're debunking whatever fad is not sensible."

That may mean creating new spins on the information as well. For example, a piece on weight loss might include a list of tips to ingest fewer calories; a story on arthritis might include a quiz to test your risk for developing it as you get older. As Littman says, a lot of health reporting covers the same basic information, so work hard to make it fresh—and better yet, memorable.

Target Your Market

As with any article, your approach to a health story will depend on the market you're pitching to. Does it run a lot of investigative articles? Is the focus on traditional medicine or alternative health? Do they prefer longer articles or shorter pieces with many sidebars? Do the stories include a lot of anecdotes, or "real people" sources, or are most of the sources experts?

Make sure that the idea and the angle you're pitching is targeted to that specific market. For example, a magazine aimed at young women probably won't be interested in a feature-length piece on osteoporosis. A parenting magazine might prefer articles about common children's health maladies like colds, ear infections, asthma, and bumps and bruises over rarer diseases that fewer readers will experience first-hand. Make sure your angle and your approach is a good fit for the magazine before you send the query.

Research, Research, Research

As mentioned previously, the most critical aspect of writing about health is being able to accurately research and report stories. That may involve tracking down articles from obscure medical journals, interviewing physicians and researchers, and making sense of medical jargon.

First stop for many health reporters is the online library for the National Institute of Medicine, which currently has more than 16 million citations. Found at www.ncbi.nlm.nih.gov/PubMed/ it can be searched by keyword, author's name, date, and other parameters. The article citations give a brief description of the type of research involved and summarize the results; you can then access the articles online or request them through your local library. Many local libraries also carry issues of major medical journals like *The Journal of the American Medical Association* ("JAMA") and *The New England Journal of Medicine*. Hospital and university libraries also have a large selection of medical journals; check your local ones to see if they grant access to writers researching stories.

While the internet has made researching health topics much easier, not all of the information you find online is accurate or even credible. However, there are a number of government health sites such as the ones for the Center for Disease Control (www.cdc.gov/), the National Institutes of Health (www.nih.gov/) and the National Center for Health Statistics (www.cdc.gov/nchs/default.htm) that every health writer should bookmark. If you find information on a site that you want to use, email to confirm that it's accurate and the most recent data the organization or agency has; you can then turn in the response along with your fact-checking material when you turn in the story.

Finding the Experts

In the world of health writing, good experts are a must—and that usually means looking beyond your own internist or pediatrician. You'll need credentialed, recognized experts to back up any claims you make, and there are many ways to find them. Professional associations such as the American Medical Association, the American College of Sports Medicine, and the American College of Obstetricians and Gynecologists all have public relations staffers who can suggest potential interviewees. Check out the Encyclopedia of Associations, a three-volume set that should be available at your local library—it includes thousands of listings for organizations, associations and groups.

You can also call the public affairs offices at major universities for recommendations or look for recent books on the subject and track down authors to request interviews. Call the publisher directly to get the author's name and number or search the web to find his or her contact info.

There are also a number of online databases that journalists can access to find experts. The largest and most popular is Profnet, found at profnet.prnewswire.com, which can be used two ways. You can search the database of experts by using keywords. Or you can submit a query, detailing the type of story you're working on and the kind of expertise you're looking for. Profnet staffers will then send your request to academic, corporate and public service sources who will contact you via phone or email if they have possible leads. While it's free for journalists, at the time of this writing, this service was only available for published freelancers. Once you get your first clips, I suggest you register and take advantage of it.

Interviewing Experts

Interviewing a medical source isn't that different from interviewing anyone else. When calling someone to arrange an interview, introduce yourself and explain who you are, the nature of the story you're working on, and why you'd like to speak with the person. Is he considered an expert in the field? Has she conducted research that you want to include in the story? It doesn't hurt to flatter someone by saying, "I've read your book and think you'd be an excellent resource for this piece,"—assuming it's true.

If the person is a doctor, ask if he or she is board-certified in any particular area; you'll also want to ask what areas an expert conducts his or her research in. Does he have a specialty? Is he affiliated with a pharmaceutical company or does he perform spokesperson work for an organization? This may affect the person's credibility and is something you need to know at the outset.

As with any interview subject, try to keep your questions open-ended. Asking "how" and "why" is a good way to delve deeper when you get short answers. Don't interrupt—make sure that the person has finished each answer before you move on. You may find that some answers provoke questions that you hadn't considered, so pay attention to what the person is saying and follow up if necessary. If your source slips into medical jargon, ask her if she can explain what she's saying "to the average person" or "so readers will understand what you mean."

At the conclusion of the interview, review your list of questions and confirm that you've covered everything you wanted to. Ask your source if he'd like to add anything or comment further. You can also inquire as to whether he's aware of anyone else—another physician or researcher, for example—who might have relevant information as well. This can be an effective way of developing additional leads.

Avoid Absolute Certainty

Finally, just as with health, remember that there are few absolutes when it comes to health writing as well. "I think in health, more than in any other writing, you need to qualify what you say," says Littman. "For example, you might write, 'this might help' or 'this may do this' because nothing works for everyone. I think you have to be more cautious about the conclusions that you draw."

Keep in mind that physicians, researchers and other experts will often disagree over even the most basic concepts ranging from the causes of disease to preventive medicine. For example, one gynecologist may feel that the health benefits of taking oral contraceptives outweighs any possible dangers, while another thinks women should avoid taking the pill entirely. Experts are entitled to their opinions, and those opinions will be influenced by their individual research areas, experiences, and beliefs. Particularly when you're writing about controversial areas, make sure that your articles address the current schools of thought. Your job as a health writer is to present a balanced picture of the information that is available—and let the reader judge for himself.

Tales from the Front: Linda Wasmer Andrews

Linda Wasmer Andrews started with a bachelor's degree in psychology and has been writing about health since the early '80s. "I've covered everything from AIDS to zoonoses [diseases that can be spread from animals to people]," says Andrews, who lives in Albuquerque, New Mexico. "Recently, I've done a lot of writing about psychiatric disorders, stress, heart disease, lung disease, and arthritis. But I've also touched on nutrition, fitness, complementary/alternative medicine, substance abuse, and a host of other topics."

Andrews' work has appeared in books, magazines, newsletters, and websites, and she has written for both consumers and health-care professionals. She says she thinks of herself as a "generalist specialist" and says that one of the keys to her success is her sincere interest in and affinity for the subject. "The bottom line is that I genuinely believe I'm helping other people," says Andrews. "While 'careers' may get stale and boring, missions last. I get a lot of satisfaction from asking myself what other people really want and need to know about keeping their bodies and minds healthy, then going to experts to find the best answers. And then trying to communicate that information in a helpful, readable way."

Andrews' advice for would-be health writers:

Take your job seriously. This is people's health you're fooling with, so you have a solemn responsibility to seek out the most reliable, up-to-date information from the most authoritative sources.

Translate doctor-speak into plain English. Talk about an ear infection, not "otitis media." Your readers are bright folks, but they may have neither the time nor the inclination to learn a whole new language.

Put news in perspective. Science moves ahead in baby steps, not giant leaps. Every development is not necessarily revolutionary or a breakthrough, and there's no such thing as a miracle cure.

Place risks in a context your readers can relate to. Offer meaningful comparisons of risks versus benefits, manmade risks versus natural ones, and unfamiliar risks versus more familiar ones.

Back up your statements with solid statistics. But avoid fuzzy phrases, such as "up to 10,000 cases," which could mean 100 or 10,000. It's better to say something like "an estimated 9,000 cases."

Cite sound research evidence. Tell your readers how large and well-controlled the study was, where it was conducted or published, and what the major implications and limitations of the data are.

Write about people, not diseases. "Don't define people by their diseases or medical status. Call a person with diabetes just that, not a diabetic or a patient," she says. "And remember that not everyone with a disease is automatically a 'victim' of it."

Finally, don't scare readers. "Of course, you want to tell the truth, even if it's grim, but you can do so tactfully. Talk about low survival rates rather than high death rates," adds Andrews. "And never leave your readers feeling helpless or hopeless. Give them practical action tips, and point them to helpful resources."

Practical Pitching:
Tips for Getting your First (or Fifteenth) Assignment

When pitching a health story, your query should include the following elements:

■ An attention-getting lead, with a time peg if possible

■ Enough information about the topic so that the editor knows why her readers will be interested

■ Details about how you will approach the story

■ An ISG that explains why you're qualified to write the piece.

For an example, look at the following query, which sold to *Woman's Day*. Note that the lead includes a recent study that demonstrates how common pelvic pain is among women of child-bearing age. The second paragraph provides additional supporting information—in addition to the one in four women with chronic pelvic pain, another one in five suffers from fibroids. The next two paragraphs flesh out the idea, but in retrospect I could have made this query even stronger by including the names of several experts I plan to interview. Finally, the ISG is weak, although for a reason—I'd written for Donna Behen before, so I didn't bother listing my clips. If I was a new writer with no clips include language like "after years of painful periods, I was diagnosed with fibroids, so I know firsthand how debilitating these conditions can be."

Dear Donna:

If you suffer from chronic pelvic pain, you're not alone. This condition is more common than most people realize—in fact, a study published last year found that 1 in 4 women of child-bearing age complain of pelvic pain that lasted more than six months.

Pelvic pain can be caused by a variety of conditions including endometriosis, fibroids, ovarian cysts, pelvic inflammatory disease, and bladder infections as well as gastrointestinal problems like irritable bowel syndrome. But many conditions may go untreated for years. For example, fibroids affect about 20% of women and are the leading cause of hysterectomies in the United States, but women may ignore symptoms like pain, bloating or heavy periods. The result is that the fibroids can continue to grow, causing other problems and often making surgery necessary. Conditions like endometriosis and pelvic inflammatory disease can also cause permanent scarring and lead to infertility if not treated early on.

Women may not realize that pelvic pain shouldn't be ignored, and this article will help them be proactive by giving them an overview of what may be causing their symptoms. If you do have pelvic pain, what are the likely causes? What symptoms should you look for? And what are the latest treatment options? Armed with this information, women will be able to take a more assertive approach to treating this problem, and improve their health in the process.

"Pain Relief for a Too-Common Problem" will explain what chronic pelvic pain is, describe the major causes and their symptoms, and provide a rundown of treatment alternatives. As with any health story, I'll interview respected medical experts and report on recent research on these conditions. I estimate a length of 2,000 words, with each condition broken out into a short section covering symptoms, cause, diagnosis and treatment; a sidebar will include a list of resources for women with these conditions.

Donna, let me know if you like the way I'm approaching this story for your "Health" section, or if you have any questions about this query. As always, thanks for your time, and I'll talk to you soon!

Best,
Kelly

The Markets: Where to Sell Your Work

Health writing offers perhaps the broadest cross-section of markets of any specialty, and rates tend to be on the high side for consumer and many trade magazines. Some of the biggest markets for health-related writing include:

General interest magazines—cover topics including new medicine, scientific breakthroughs, preventive health, alternative medicine, health policy, and other related areas.

Professional and trade journals—depending on the journal, may be narrower range of interest; some journals cover only a limited subject area. There are thousands of trade journals aimed at specific practice areas including dentistry, sports medicine, and obstetrics as well as more general ones that cover marketing, managing practices, and other business-related topics.

Women's and men's magazines—cover a broad range of health-related subjects, mostly service-oriented. Women's magazines also include profile-type pieces about people who have faced medical challenges; both men's and women's mags also cover diet and fitness topics as well. (See other chapters for more information about these specialties.)

Parenting magazines—cover children's health, nutrition, development, childhood diseases, first aid, and preventive health. Some magazines also feature women's health articles, particularly those related to conception, pregnancy, and birth.

Health and fitness magazines—similar to general interest magazines in terms of coverage, addressing nearly every health-related topic. These markets tend to be aimed at more specialized audiences, however—women in their 20s and 30s for example, or men and women 50 and up—so keep that in mind when pitching stories.

Cooking/food magazines—again, there's a lot of crossover between nutrition and health-related subjects. Many of these magazines will cover health topics, often focusing on preventive health.

Science magazines—while they have a narrower range of interest, these markets often cover breakthroughs in medical technology or other new research findings.

Health-oriented web sites—these markets cover a variety of health topics. As with other online publications, stories tend to run shorter than in print markets and include quizzes, links to other sites and other interactive features.

Specialty publications—these markets are aimed at people who have a specific disease or condition like arthritis, diabetes, or cancer.

More limited area of interest, but still cover a wide range of topics with an emphasis on service to readers.

Custom publications—these magazines, aimed at a limited audience, often cover health from a wellness or lifestyle angle. Focus is again often of prevention rather than cure.

National/major newspapers—cover a wide range of health topics.

Regional/city magazines and newspapers—like their national counterparts, regional and city publications also cover a broad range of health-related topics, many with a local angle.

In addition to markets looking for articles, there is a variety of other opportunities for writers who specialize in health, including freelancing for pharmaceutical companies, hospitals, and public relations agencies. Many writers also cover medical conferences and other events or develop regular beats in particular areas of health and medicine.

Other Useful Stuff

As already mentioned, in the field of health, it's important to keep up on the newest developments. The more access you have to what's going on, the better. Sign up for email news releases from sites like PRNewswire and newsdesk.com, which will update you on newly published studies and research. You can also register for email lists and get on the press lists for medical organizations, colleges, and universities which will notify you about breaking news.

As a health writer, you may find these sources helpful for sources, data, and other relevant information:

Online Resources:

InteliHealth, www.intelihealth.com. Offers free email newsletters on a variety of health-related topics; website also includes basic health information.

PRNewswire, www.prnmedia.com. PRNewswire (which also hosts Profnet) provides email newsletters and news releases on healthcare subjects; you can search the site for releases on specific topics.

Newswise, www.newswise.com. Newswise offers free email newsletters on health topics; also maintains an online directory of experts.

Profnet, profnet.prnewswire.com. Search the online database or submit a query to find experts in particular areas; you must be a published freelancer and register to use the services.

PubMed; www.ncbi.nlm.nih.gov/PubMed/. PubMed provides online access to the National Library of Medicine, and includes links to a variety of health websites.

Reuters Health, www.reutershealth.com/. Site includes daily news releases about health, medicine and nutrition.

Government Agencies

Centers for Disease Control and Prevention
Headquarters: 1600 Clifton Road, N.E.
Atlanta, GA 30333
404-639-3534 or 800-311-3435
www.cdc.gov

The CDC surveys worldwide disease trends, epidemics and environmental health problems, maintains statistics, and promotes preventive health.

Health and Human Services Department
200 Independence Ave., S.W. #615F
Washington, D.C. 20201
Phone: 202-690-7000, press inquiries 202-690-6343
www.hhs.gov

The HHS encompasses the Health Care Financing Administration, the Administration for Children and Families, the Public Health Service, and the Centers for Disease Control.

National Center for Health Statistics
6525 Belcrast Road #1140
Hyattsville, MD 20782
Phone: 301-458-4500, press inquiries 301-458-4800
www.cdc.gov/nchs/default.htm

The NCHS compiles, analyzes, and disseminates national and international statistics on all matters pertaining to health.

National Institutes of Health
1 Center Dr., Building 1 #126
Bethesda, Md. 20892-0148
Phone: 301-496-2433, press 301-496-4461
www.nih.gov

The National Institutes of Health promote and conduct biomedical research into the causes and prevention of diseases and furnish information to health professionals and the public.

Other Associations/Organizations

American College of Sports Medicine

401 W. Michigan St.
Indianapolis, IN 46202-3233
Phone: 317-637-9200
www.acsm.org

This 20,000-member organization integrates scientific research, education and practical applications of sports medicine and exercise science to maintain and improve physical performance, fitness, health, and quality of life. The ACSM also certifies fitness and exercise specialists and instructors.

American Medical Association

515 N. State St.
Chicago, IL 60610
Phone: 312-464-5000
www.ama-assn.org

The AMA is the largest medical organization in the country, consisting of 297,000 medical doctors. The AMA publishes *The Journal of the American Medical Association* and disseminates scientific information to members and the public.

American Psychiatric Association

1400 K Street, N.W.
Washington, D.C. 20005
Phone: 202-682-6000, press inquiries 202-682-6142
www.psych.org

This 35,000-member organization consists solely of psychiatrists and provides press referrals for experts.

American Psychological Association

750 First Street, N.E.
Washington, D.C. 20002-4242
Phone: 202-336-5510 or 800-374-2721
www.apa.org

This 150,000-member association promotes psychology as a science, profession and means of helping humanity; good source for psychology experts.

American Public Health Association
800 I St. N.W.
Washington, D.C. 20001
Phone: 202-777-2742
www.apha.org
This association consists of health care professionals, educators, environmentalists, social workers, industrial hygienists, and individuals; maintains information on all aspects of health care and education and conducts research on the causes and origin of communicable diseases.

Institute for Health Care Research and Policy
2233 Wisconsin Ave., N.W. #525
Washington, D.C. 20007
Phone: 202-687-0880
www.georgetown.edu/research/ihcrp/
The institute is a research branch of Georgetown University and includes interests in quality care, cost effectiveness, managed care, health privacy and access to care.

Writers' Organizations and Other Resources:

American Medical Writers Association
40 West Guide Drive Suite 101
Rockville, MD 20850-1192
Phone: 301-294-5303
www.amwa.org
This 5,300-member organization includes medical writers, editors, public relations and pharmaceutical personnel, educators, publishers and others concerned with communications in medicine and allied sciences; holds an annual conference and publishes a directory of members available for freelance work.

Association of Health Care Journalists
Missouri School of Journalism, 10 Neff Hall
Columbia, MO 65211
Phone: 573-884-5606
www.healthjournalism.org/
The 950-member association is an independent nonprofit association for health care writers.

National Association of Science Writers
P.O. Box 890
Hedgeville, WV 25427
Phone: 304-754-5077
www.nasw.org
This 2,450-member organization includes writers and editors of science news for the public; holds annual conference and includes some helpful info for freelancers on its website.

Book

Health Writer's Handbook, by Barbara Gastel, M.D. (Iowa State University Press, 1998); excellent guide to writing about health.

From Bananas to Blintzes:
Writing About Diet, Nutrition and Food

According to the U.S. Centers for Disease Control, a whopping two-thirds of adult Americans are now classified as overweight—and that figure continues to grow, pardon the pun. Not surprisingly, every year a new crop of diet books arrives in bookstores, and quick weight-loss plans have long been popular in women's, men's and fitness magazines, and will continue to be so. Yet Americans also love to read about—and enjoy—food, whether it's a gourmet meal for two, a simple family meal, or a backyard barbecue for the whole gang.

There's more to writing about nutrition than simply describing the latest fad diet and whether it works. There is also a growing interest in articles about how nutrition can improve your health, reduce your risk of disease, and even impact your mood and well-being. More specialized fields like sports nutrition and geriatric nutrition are also gaining attention. Food writing—whether it's developing recipes aimed at middle-class families living on budgets or running down the latest cooking trend for higher-end gourmands—is another lucrative area for those who specialize in it. If you have experience in any of these areas—or if you just love food—this may be a specialty for you to consider.

Keep in mind, though, that a love of food may give you story ideas, but to get assignments, you need to show the editor why you're uniquely qualified to write the piece. That's where your ISG comes into play again. Let's say you're a vegetarian whose meatless meals please even the carnivores in your life. Some possible story ideas might include:

■ An article for a parenting magazine on what to do when your child announces she's no longer going to eat meat

■ A story for a local magazine that lists restaurants that specialize in vegetarian cuisine

■ A short piece for a fitness magazine on the latest in meat substitutes, their protein content, and their pros and cons

■ An article for a women's magazines on how to whip up some delicious meatless appetizers for a holiday party

■ A story that uses a lead about recent research on fiber intake and how adding more vegetables and grains to your diet can help with weight loss.

That's just a start. And don't just consider traditional food magazines; many publications cover food, nutrition, and diet topics. Start with what you know best, and when writing your ISG, make sure you include any information that will help convince the editor to give you the story, whether you're on a low-salt diet and are writing about salt substitutes or just won a chili cooking contest and are pitching a piece on backyard cookouts.

Nuts and Bolts: How to Write about Diet, Nutrition and Food

Build Your Background
While it doesn't hurt, it takes more than the ability to whip together a delicious homemade dinner in less than ten minutes to be a successful food or nutrition writer. Some people are great cooks who can't write; some (like myself, actually) are great writers who can't cook. If you lack any specialized background in this area, you may want to develop it before you begin pitching ideas.

"If you're writing about food, cook and learn about food," says freelancer Claire Walter of Boulder, Colorado, who writes about food, snow sports and travel. "So if writing restaurant reviews is going to become your specialty, it's not a bad thing to spend a little time getting a job in a restaurant, to get a behind-the-scenes look at whatever your field is." If you've worked in a restaurant, attended a culinary institute or been a chef, you have a leg up on other freelancers. Even reading a few basic books on food and nutrition can help give you a handle on cooking techniques, what nutrients like vitamins and minerals are, and basic terminology.

By the way, for all you would-be restaurant critics, let me give you the bad news. It's not as simple as sampling the latest eatery's dishes and reporting on how delicious they tasted. "First of all, restaurant reviewers rarely get paid all that much," says freelancer Erik Sherman, who writes about food, technology, and business. "If you're going to review restaurants in general, then you need to do it well…It's a matter of understanding what the concept of the restaurant is, what the demands of the particular cuisine are, and whether the dishes are done correctly or not. You have to be able to write from that perspective. It's not a matter of 'I liked this or I didn't like this.'"

Consider the Audience

When you're coming up with story ideas, think about the purpose of your story before you write the query or the article itself. Will it be a service-oriented piece explaining why readers should eat more omega-3 and omega-6 fats, and offer ways to incorporate foods that contain them into their diets? An article comparing the quality of mail-order steaks from different companies? A story on the latest pinot noirs, and the best value $20 bottle of wine? Or a round-up of recipes aimed at busy moms?

Also consider the audience you're writing for. If you're doing a piece on five new ways to prepare chicken for a magazine like *Family Circle*, you'll probably focus on ease of preparation, low ingredient cost, and taste that both adults and children will like. For a piece for *Gourmet*, however, you'll want to take a more upscale approach both in terms of the ingredients themselves and in the cooking and preparation.

Consider the terms you use as well. Readers of *Food & Wine* know the difference between mincing, slicing, and julienning; non-foodies may not. If there's any doubt, include the definitions of terms you use, whether you're referring to a cooking method or ingredient. Your readers (and your editor) will thank you.

Think Seasonal

This may be obvious to those who spend time in the kitchen, but a lot of food-based writing is seasonally oriented. Obviously most people don't want to spend hours in the kitchen making hearty soups and stews during the hottest months of the year, and during the winter months, some fruits and vegetables may be more difficult to come by. Coming up with a holiday or seasonal theme for your articles, whether it's Christmas, St. Patrick's Day, Halloween, or Lent—or for graduations, picnics, or tailgates—will also increase your chance of selling the idea.

That's why you should keep lead time in mind. When do the holidays appear on your radar? In November? That's way too late. You should be pitching your Christmas cookie roundup idea as early as March or April. Magazines that cover food are always looking for seasonal tie-ins, so keep that in mind, and make sure that you're thinking not of next month, but six months in the future. And look for a fresh viewpoint or a new angle on a tried-and-true topic to get your foot in the door. Instead of a story on the ubiquitous green bean casserole for Thanksgiving, why not suggest a piece on three other ways to prepare green beans—or better yet, four new vegetable side dishes to liven up the groaning board?

Stay Trendy

Foods come in and out of fashion just like clothing styles. The low-carb diet movement has lost momentum, but there are still plenty of people counting carb grams while others grab every low-fat and no-fat item they can find. Some of us are interested in eating foods in their natural state, while others are trying to eliminate all sugar from their diets. Others are enjoying a return to the "comfort foods" they grew up with. Stay in touch with what's hot both in diets and food, and use that information to pitch timely story ideas.

Reading food service magazines that are aimed at restaurant owners and food packagers will give you an idea of new trends breaking through for a consumer audience. Watch for hot ingredients, sauces, and cooking styles. Attending food shows, talking to local chefs, and reading food-related blogs will help you keep up on new ingredients and cooking styles.

Do Your Homework

If you've spent years in the kitchen, or measuring every morsel you put in your mouth, you probably know more about food than the average person. Don't let that fact go to your head—when writing about nutrition, it's important to "know what you don't know," says Ed Blonz, a researcher and nutrition writer in Kensington, California. "I find that nutrition is something that everyone feels a sense of familiarity with because we all eat," says Blonz. "And also, there's a logic involved with 'this is good' and 'this is bad.' Without understanding the science behind it, people can get the mindset that they have more a grasp than they do, so not knowing the limits of your knowledge might lead you to accept basic intuitive explanations that have no scientific validity."

That's why most editors will insist that you back up any nutrition claims with copies of studies, research articles and the like. Keep in mind that just as there are no "miracle cures," there are no miracle ingredients either. Sure, some nutrients are better for you, but be skeptical about any claims you hear. If you don't have a background in nutrition and don't know the difference between Olestra and isoflavones, invest in a textbook that covers the basics; you might also take an entry-level nutrition course at your local college.

The knowledge you gather will make you a more knowledgeable—and skeptical—researcher and writer. When you're researching stories, be wary of any claims that sound too good to be true. "Be careful with the Internet," says Blonz. "It's fraught with commercial interests that are being masked as unbiased information." So how do you separate fact from fiction and helpful information from hype? By asking your sources to back up any claims they make. If you interview a researcher who says that his study proves that adding red pepper to food can help you lose weight, press for details about his work. What kind of study was involved? Where were the results published? How much red pepper was used? How much weight did people lose? Were the study subjects even human? (You'd be amazed at the number of nutrition studies cited as conclusive by some experts that turn out to involve rats or other animals.)

Find the Experts

It helps to start developing a list of expert sources who know what's happening in the field. Associations like the American Dietetic Association will give you referrals to registered dietitians who have backgrounds in particular areas; you can also check with local colleges and universities to learn what types of research they're conducting. If you're working on a story and need an expert, call a major university or hospital and ask for their public affairs department; they can usually hook you up with a qualified person.

"Read as much as you can of other writers and scientists who are doing what you want to do," says Blonz. "You start getting an idea of who's who. Every time you see someone who is saying something that makes sense, write their name down, and you'll start to compile lists of sources for the various aspects of nutrition and food."

Be Daring

A basic grasp of nutrition and an ability to translate research studies will give you a leg up if you're interested in writing about general nutrition. However, writing about food itself (as opposed to its nutrients) isn't for everyone—if you're a vegetarian or even a picky eater, you might want to consider another specialty. To write about food, you have to keep an open mind about new tastes, cooking styles, and trends. Whether you're developing recipes or reviewing restaurants, you've got to be willing to put your taste buds to the test.

"You have to be daring, and I think anyone who wants to write about food is," says Walter. "You can't turn your nose up at vast categories of cooking, and I would suspect that anyone who doesn't have an adventuresome palate won't want to write about food anyway."

Be careful of your own biases, too. While I'm a vegetarian, I've written plenty of articles that talk about the nutritional benefits of eating beef, for example. I can't let my personal preferences overshadow the writing and reporting I do. While I might not believe all of the claims that some of the fad diet stories I've written promise, I can still report and write the story, and leave it up for readers to try and judge on their own.

Get Out of the House

If you do a lot of food or recipe writing, you may spend a lot of time in your own kitchen developing and test recipes. But attending meetings or seminars can help you stay abreast of what's happening in the fields of nutrition and food, and may help you nail more work as well. "Network, network, network," says Walter. "You never know where referrals will come from, and you never know who will call because you met at a conference or because you were both at a workshop."

If you've got more of a reputation for covering topics other than food, make sure your editors and clients know that you write about the latter as well. Erik Sherman's new book, *The Complete Idiot's Guide to International Pizza and Panini,* was the result of a casual conversation with an editor he was already working for. "I'd done *The Complete Idiot's Guide to Photography,* and hit the deadlines and she mentioned they were going to do this [book]," he says. "I'd never done a cookbook but I'd done a little bit of food writing, and the point was they knew I could write." Sherman mentioned several recipes he'd include in such a cookbook—like brie and artichoke Panini—and eventually nabbed the book deal.

Be Clear

Articles about food and nutrition must also be accurate and easy to understand. Be as specific as you can—if you're writing about fiber, don't just say "it's important to include more fiber in your diet," for example. Instead, say "most dietitians recommend that adults eat between 25 and 35 grams of fiber a day." Then give ways that readers can do that, or include examples of how much fiber common foods contain.

Obviously, when writing recipes, you must specify the exact amounts of ingredients. List them in the order they are used, and include any special cooking or preparation tools—nonstick pans, for example—as well as a list of the steps to take to put the recipe together. Make things easy, concise, and clear. If you have any questions, have someone who doesn't spend time in the kitchen read through your recipe. If your reader has questions, chances are your editor will, too.

Tales From the Front: Monica Bhide

Monica Bhide "focuses on food and culture and their effect on our lives," says the Dunnloring, Virginia-based freelancer. She's only been freelancing fulltime for three years, but has amassed impressive clips in publications ranging from *The New York Times* to *Gourmet* and *Food & Wine*. Her advice to writers who want to crack this market:

Expand your horizons. Bhide started out writing primarily about Indian food, but quickly realized she needed to expand her subject area to get more assignments. "Now I write about anything and everything related to the food industry," she says. "I have a piece in *Health* magazine about what to do with Thanksgiving leftovers, I did a piece for *The Washington Post* on the types of saki that are available, and I did a piece for *Wine Enthusiast* on a chef who's crazy about honey…if you're going to specialize in this industry, people really need to broaden their idea of what an industry means."

Think broadly—not only in terms of subject matter, but audiences. Study potential markets and make sure you understand their audiences, and the demographics of those audiences. As the mother of a young son, Bhide writes about food for kids, but she's also writes food-related articles for AARP's website. An ability to write for such diverse audiences will make you more marketable.

Decide which aspect of food writing appeals to you. For example, there's service-oriented writing ("here are the types of cheese on the market and here's what you should try and why"), health-oriented food/nutrition stories (the impact trans fatty acids have on your stomach), in addition to food-related essays. "Drill it down to what it is that you want to do," says Bhide. "Do you want write about the taste and texture of food? Do you want to do reporting? Do you want to be an investigative person? Pick a topic…and read a lot [of what] you want to write."

Provide plenty of detail. Don't skimp on your query letters, especially as a new writer. For her first sale to *The New York Times*, Bhide wound up expanding her original query to one that was five pages long, and included details about the types of sources she would contact. With only a few clips, she nailed a major feature on the impact India's growing economy was affecting the Indian food industry—because she was able to demonstrate her knowledge of the subject when the editor called her to discuss it. "I researched the story inside and out," she says. "He could ask me questions and I could tell him why I was the one to write the story, what the angle was, and why it was relevant today."

Pitch specific angles. Too many writers will pitch an idea like, "oh, I'm going to Spain, and I want to write about it," say Bhide. A better approach? Pitch a story on the special dogs they train to hunt truffles during Spain's truffle season in May. "The devil is in the details," says Bhide. The more specific and unique your idea is—assuming it's a good fit for the market—the better chance you have of making the sale.

Practical Pitching:
Tips for Getting Your First (or Fifteenth) Assignment

When pitching a food, nutrition, or diet story, your query should include the following elements:
- An attention-getting lead, with a time peg if possible
- Enough information about the topic so that the editor knows why her readers will be interested
- Details about how you will approach the story
- An ISG that explains why you're qualified to write the piece

For an example, look at the following query, which sold to *Oxygen*, a diet and fitness magazine. The anecdotal lead is something that most women can relate to, although I could have used a real person rather than a general statement to make it more compelling. In the second paragraph, I cite a couple of recent studies which give a time peg, show that food cravings are quite common among women (who also happen to be *Oxygen's* audience), and that food cravings can be overcome. The third paragraph explains how I'll approach the story, gives an idea of the caliber of experts I plan to interview (in fact, I did use Debra Waterhouse for the piece), and a possible sidebar. Finally, in the ISG, I suggest the section of the magazine the story is appropriate for, and highlight my clips and personal experience with food cravings. This is a pretty good query, and one that just about any new freelancer could write.

Dear Nancy:

You'd been doing great on your healthy eating plan, sticking to lean protein, whole grains, and lots of fruits and veggies. That was, until this afternoon, at 4 p.m., when you were overcome with a raging, uncontrollable urge for a king-sized Snickers bar. You tried to distract yourself, but eventually gave in—and then felt guilty.

If your diet has been derailed by food cravings, you're not alone. One recent study found that 85% of women surveyed had experienced food cravings at least once in the past three months. Another study found that more than one-quarter of women describe themselves as "cravers" who experience a strong urge to eat specific foods more than once a week. But food cravings aren't intrinsically evil—they may simply be the result of too-strict dieting or indicate a lack of certain nutrients. Women may also be biologically programmed to experience food cravings, which should make you feel a little better when you're driving to the 7-11 late at night because there's no chocolate in the house.

"Conquer your Food Cravings: What They Mean and How to Overcome Them" will explain why women experience these intense desires for certain foods, and offer ways of combating them. I'll report on recent research, and plan to interview experts such as registered dietitian and nutritionist Debra Waterhouse, author of Outsmarting the Female Fat Cell After Pregnancy (Hyperion, 2002) and Why Women Need Chocolate (Hyperion, 1995), for this story. While I estimate 1500 words, that's flexible depending on your needs; a possible sidebar will include a list of "most-craved foods."

Interested in this story for your "Nutrition" section? I'm a full-time freelancer who's written for magazines including Fitness, Self, Shape, Marie Claire, Cosmopolitan, Woman's Day, and Fit; I'm also a fitness buff and self-admitted chocoholic with a first-hand understanding of food cravings. I hope you'll find this story appropriate for a future issue of Oxygen; please let me know if you have questions about it.

Thanks very much for your time and consideration; I look forward to hearing from you soon.

Best,
Kelly James-Enger

The Markets: Where to Sell Your Work

Write about diet, nutrition, and food, and you'll find a wide variety of markets for your work. Some of the biggest include:

Cooking/food magazines—there are a variety of these magazines aimed at everyone from gourmands to vegetarians. All cover cooking techniques, food trends, nutrition research, and other related subjects.

General interest magazines—encompass a broad range of topics including new breakthroughs in nutrition, research, food trends, cooking techniques and other related areas.

Trade journals—trade journals aimed at food professionals vary in their coverage, but may be markets for the latest developments in nutrition and food. Trade magazines aimed at other industries such as those involving fitness and health also feature nutrition and food articles.

Women's and men's magazines—these magazines cover a broad range of food, nutrition and diet subjects, mostly service-oriented.

Parenting magazines—all cover children's nutrition and related topics; many feature simple recipes, topics like packing healthier lunches, cooking with kids, and the like.

Health and fitness magazines—similar to general interest magazines in terms of coverage—broad scope of nearly every nutrition-related topic. These markets tend to be aimed at more specialized audiences, however—women in their 20s and 30s for example, or men and women 50 and up—so keep that in mind when pitching stories.

Travel magazines—many travel magazines include articles on the foods and cultures of different places; writing about food and travel is a natural combination.

Websites—many web sites, not just health sites, cover a variety of health topics. As with other online publications, stories tend to run shorter than in print markets and include quizzes, links to other sites and other interactive features.

National/major magazines—all have food, nutrition and/or cooking sections.

Regional/city magazines and newspapers—like their national counterparts, regional and city publications also cover food and nutrition subjects, many with a local angle.

Other Useful Stuff

When researching stories about food, nutrition and diet subjects, you'll need to find and interview credentialed, reliable experts and research studies. Some of the organizations and governmental agencies that can provide you with that kind of information and experts are listed below:

Online Resources

Food Dictionary of Cooking Terms at Epicurious.com, www.epi-curious.com/cooking/how_to/food_dictionary. Dictionary that includes more than 4,000 cooking terms.

InteliHealth, www.intelihealth.com. Offers free email newsletters on nutrition and related topics; website also includes basic nutrition information.

Newswise, www.newswise.com. Newswise offers free email newsletters, maintains press releases and an online directory of experts.

Profnet, profnet.prnewswire.com. Search the online database or submit a query to find experts in particular areas; you must be a published freelancer and register to use the service.

PubMed, www.ncbi.nlm.nih.gov/PubMed/. PubMed provides online access to the National Library of Medicine.

Reuters Health, www.reutershealth.com/. Site that includes daily news releases about health, medicine and nutrition.

Tufts University Health & Nutrition Letter, healthletter.tufts-.edu/home2.htm. Well-respected newsletter covers nutrition and health.

Government Agencies

Agricultural Research Service (part of USDA)
1400 Independence Ave, S.W. Suite 302A
Washington, D.C. 20250-0300
Phone: 202-720-3656
Website: www.ars.usda.gov
This is a nationwide network of research centers that study human nutrition, livestock and crop production, protection and processing.

Cooperative State Research, Education and Extension Service (Agriculture Dept.)
1400 Independence Ave., S.W. #305A
Washington, D.C. 20250-2201
Phone: 202-720-4423
Website: www.reeusdda.gov
This agency oversees county agents and operation of state offices that provide information on nutrition, diet, food purchase budgeting, food safety, home gardening and other consumer concerns.

FDA Center for Food Safety and Applied Nutrition

5100 Paint Branch Parkway
College Park, MD 20740-3835
Phone 1-888-723-3366 (CFSAN Food and Information Center)
Website: www.cfsan.fda.gov

The FDA's Center for Food Safety and Applied Nutrition monitors the safety and labeling of food and cosmetic products. The FDA itself is responsible for developing standards of composition and quality of foods (except meat and poultry); its website is www.fda.gov.

National Agricultural Library

Food and Nutrition Information Center
10301 Baltimore Avenue #105
Beltsville, MD 20705-2351
Phone: 301-504-5719
Website: www.nal.usda.gov/fnic

The center serves individuals and agencies seeking information or educational materials on food and human nutrition, provides reference services and develops resource lists of health and nutrition publications.

Other Associations/Organizations

American Dietetic Association (ADA)

216 W. Jackson Boulevard
Chicago, IL 60606-6995
Phone: 312-899-0040
eatright.org

This 65,000-member organization is made up of registered dietitians, dietetic technicians and other professionals. The ADA promotes nutrition, health and well-being and publishes the *Journal of the American Dietetic Association*; it also offers nutritional and statistical information to journalists and refers to ADA spokespersons for expert sources.

American Society for Nutrition

9650 Rockville Pike, Suite L-4500
Bethesda, MD 20814
Phone 301-634-7050
www.nutrition.org

This organization includes more than 3,500 members and supports research on the role of human nutrition in health and disease.

Center for Science in the Public Interest
1875 Connecticut Avenue NW #300
Washington, D.C. 20009-5728
Phone: 202-332-9110
www.cspinet.org

This organization conducts research on food and nutrition; interests include eating habits, food safety regulations, food additives, organically produced foods, alcohol beverages and links between diet and disease.

International Food Information Council
1100 Connecticut Avenue, N.W. #430
Washington, D.C. 20036
Phone: 202-296-6540
www.ific.org

This organization includes food and beverage companies and manufacturers of food ingredients; provides the media, health professionals, and consumers with scientific information about food safety, health and nutrition.

National Restaurant Association
1200 17th St., NW
Washington, D.C. 20036
Phone: 202-331-5900
www.restaurant.org

This trade organization consists of more than 50,000 member companies representing more than 254,000 restaurants; maintains statistics.

Physicians Committee for Responsible Medicine
5100 Wisconsin Avenue, N.W. #400
Washington, D.C. 20016
www.pcrm.org

This organization is made up of health care professionals, medical students and laypersons interested in preventive medicine; and conducts clinical research, educational programs and public info campaigns.

Society for Nutrition Education
7150 Winton Drive, Suite 300
Indianapolis, IN 46268
Phone: 317-328-4627 or 800-235-6690
www.sne.org

This group includes nutrition educators from the fields of dietetics, public health, home economics, medicine, industry and education.

Writers' Organizations

Association of Food Journalists
38309 Genesee Lake Road
Oconomowac, WI 53066
Phone: 262-965-3251
www.afjonline.com
   This 275-member organization includes both freelance food journalists and those on staff at newspapers, magazines, and internet services.

International Association of Culinary Professionals
304 W. Liberty St., Suite 201
Louisville, KY 40202
Phone 502-581-9786 or 800-928-4227
www.iacp.com/
   This 4,000-member organization includes food writers, cookbook authors, cooking school owners, chefs, caterers, teachers, food stylists and photographers.

International Food, Wine and Travel Writers Association
1142 South Diamond Bar Boulevard #177
Diamond Bar, CA 91765
Phone: 877-439-8929
www.ifwtwa.org
   This 300-member organization consists of professional food, wine and travel journalists in 28 countries.

Books

   The Recipe Writer's Handbook, Revised and Updated, by Barbara Gibbs Ostmann and Jane Baker (Wiley, 2001); includes info on recipe-writing and tons of helpful resources.
   The Resource Guide for Food Writers, by Gary Allen (Routledge, 1999); loaded with organizations, periodicals, web sites, databases and other sources of information for food and nutrition writers.
   Will Write for Food: The Complete Guide to Writing Cookbooks, Restaurant Reviews, Articles, Memoir, Fiction and More, by Dianne Jacob (Marlowe & Co., 2005); explains how to get started in every area of food writing; includes writing exercises and marketing ideas.

Show Me the Money:
Writing About Business and Finance

Write well about business and you'll find no shortage of markets for your work—general interest magazines, in-flight magazines, financial-oriented publications, newspapers and websites are some of the many outlets for stories about business, trade, and commerce. In addition, tens of thousands of trade journals are actively looking for free-lance writers who can report on their industries and translate the latest developments in local, national and international business to readers.

The consumer finance area is another growing field for freelancers with stories that run the gamut from how newlyweds can communicate about money to how to save for your children's college education to smart investment strategies for the future. While it doesn't hurt to have a background in business or finance, any writer with experience in a particular industry or profession can use that knowledge to crack these rewarding markets and create his or her own niche.

When I teach magazine writing, I quiz my students about the jobs they have (or have had), and encourage them to start their freelance careers by pitching trade magazines. Trade magazines are often overlooked by writers, and that's a mistake—they don't receive as many queries as consumer magazines, and they are usually more willing to work with a new writer, provided that person knows their industry or business. Take Alida Zamboni, whose first query is included in chapter 3. She used her nursing background to pitch a statewide nursing magazine about the impact of a new law. She could have pitched other ideas to other markets, including:

■ A piece for a parenting magazine on how to get faster care in the emergency room

■ A story for a fitness magazine about the most common sports-related injuries that require medical treatment and how to prevent them

■ A short piece on how long over-the-counter medications and prescription drugs retain their potency

■ An article for a general interest publication on the nursing shortage and the reasons behind it

■ A piece on interviewing techniques for a trade publication for emergency medicine technicians (in fact, this was Zamboni's second article sale!)

Whether you pitch trade or consumer magazines, start with an aspect of business you already know something about. National business magazines can be difficult to break into, so you may want to focus on smaller or regional publications to garner your first clips.

Nuts and Bolts: How to Write about Business and Finance

Don't be Afraid

First things first. What if you want to write about business, but are worried you don't know enough about it? While there is a learning curve involved, it's not as complicated as you may think. "I think a lot of reporters are scared of business writing—I find I get a lot of work because there aren't as many people out there who feel comfortable writing about business," says freelancer Margaret Littman of Chicago, who writes about business and health subjects. "Yes, business writing is technical and you have to know what you're talking about—you have know what an earnings statement is, for example, and know what the terminology is, but people think of it is a niche and it's not. Everyone runs a business or works for a business. Every business issue affects almost everyone."

If you're still feeling under-qualified to pitch business subjects, start with subjects you already have some background in. For example, one of the first business articles I sold was on how small business owners could avoid employment discrimination claims. As an attorney in private practice, my work included defending small companies in discrimination cases, so I was comfortable writing about the subject. On the other hand, I would have had no idea how to approach a story on viral marketing or tax shelters for small companies, so I stuck with what I knew.

Use Your Experience

I'm not the only writer to use a background in a particular business or industry to get started in this field. Joshua Karp, a writer based in Evanston, Illinois, was finishing his master's degree in journalism when he nabbed his first business story. He had worked in advertising and marketing as well as for a manufacturing and distribution company before returning to school, and used that fact to help convince an editor at *Crain's Chicago Business* to give him an assignment. The first assignment turned into others, and by the time he graduated, he was doing two stories a month for the publication.

Karp's next regular gig was for a dotcom where he wrote a 700-word piece on high-tech business once a week. "I got to pick my beat and I chose to cover high-tech business. I worked for them for six months, basically covering the intersection between creativity and technology," says Karp. "That was a great experience. It was great to get the money and to have the work, but I also got to grow a lot as a business writer." He covered topics including video production, web design, and advertising, and in just a few months' time, had developed an expertise in business and technology. In the years since then, he's continued writing about business but has branched into writing profiles as well. Blending the two led to his first book, *A Futile and Stupid Gesture: How Doug Kenney and National Lampoon Changed Comedy Forever* (Chicago Review Press, 2006).

Know Your Stuff

When you're writing about business, you have to be a thorough researcher—it's not enough to talk to only one person about a particular topic. Remember that your readers are going to have a vested interest in the subject and often already know a lot about the topics you're writing about. If you're missing critical information or don't understand a concept, don't try to write around it and hope readers won't notice. You have to understand it or your ignorance will be reflected in your stories—and people will notice. "You don't want to get caught with your pants down," warns Karp. "I find with business there are a lot of angles and you've got to make sure that you're getting the core of what people are saying...if you don't get it, it really comes through."

Instead, start with the aspects of business you already know and expand your knowledge base from there. If some part of what you're writing about is a brand new topic for you, get some basic guidebooks and reference books to educate yourself about what you're covering. You can learn along the way without looking stupid. My first business articles were on contracts and employment discrimination claims. As I gained experience, I started writing for several trade magazines, covering other employment-related subjects like meeting management and employee incentive programs. As you develop familiarity with one area of business, it's easier to move into others.

Don't be Afraid to Be Creative

Think business stories have to be as exciting as watching paint dry? Think again—and strive to enhance your stories with creativity whenever possible. "Business stories don't need to be dry, boring stuff," agrees Kristin Baird Rattini, a freelancer who writes for trade and custom publications in addition to consumer magazines. Rattini does a lot of profiles of small business owners, and admits that it can be challenging to come up with a new approach to each one. Still, she always looks for something that makes the story unique. Consider a story she was assigned on a new paint line where she had to interview a True Value retailer in southwest Utah who was selling the paint.

"It could have been a very dry story—'this is the paint,' 'this is how they're selling it', et cetera," says Rattini. "But because of the retailer's location in the Wild, Wild West and because of a confrontational encounter he had with another paint retailer in town, I was able to spin it with a Wild West theme and really add creativity and flair to it. It's up to you to find the creative potential in each story and know that you don't have to do a rote, boring, dry business story just because it seems like a boring topic initially."

Karp too seeks to have some kind of story line running through his articles. "I want it to have as much of a narrative flow as humanly possible," he says. "At the very least, it should have a lead and an ending and some kind of narrative flow that runs from one end to the other with a lot of reporting in the middle." He also likes to surprise his readers. For example, in one of his articles on home offices, he used a lead that described a huge corporate office fully equipped with the latest in cutting-edge technology. In closing the lead, he noted that there were also toys and Cheerios strewn about on the floor—the business owner's office is located in her daughter's nursery.

Pitch New—and Tried and True—Story Ideas

One of the best ways to come up with story ideas is to track what local companies are doing and watch for business trends. Talk to your local chamber of commerce, read the business section of the local papers, and keep your ears open for possible subjects. For stories on personal finance topics, evergreen subjects like credit cards, saving for retirement, and investment "dos "and "don'ts" never go out of style. Look at what financial issues your own family is facing or the topics you talk about with your friends.

"There's an endless well of stories out there being run on credit cards, credit card debt, and saving for college. They're perennial stories because families grow into the stories every year and there's always a market for those topics," says Rattini. "Consumer finance is something that is both familiar and foreign. It's familiar because we may be going through it on our own but we may not understand what we're going through. Look at what you're experiencing personally to find some ideas, and at the very least, some lessons to work from."

Be Extra Accurate

When you're writing about business, you can't fudge numbers or guess when you should have specific data. If your stories include mistakes, you'll have a short-lived career as a business writer; on the other hand, if you develop a reputation for accuracy, you'll have no shortage of work. Even simple mistakes can trip you up—miscalculating a percentage, for example.

It may be basic math, but double-check your work and let your editor know how you came up with any figures (the editor will want to know the sources of any data you cite anyway). And if experts quote figures or statistics, ask them where the numbers came from and how they were calculated. Remember the old saying: "figures don't lie, but liars can figure."

Know the Style Book

Business publications in particular tend to be fussy about their style books. A style book, or style guidelines, refers to the rules that a publisher follows to maintain consistent writing—such as how common words are abbreviated and which rules of punctuation are followed. Many publications use either Chicago or AP style, although *The New York Times* insists on having its own. AP style is commonly accepted as the standard for news writing, and is often used by business magazines as well.

The real issue is being able to follow the style book of the publication you're pitching. How does the magazine identify people in articles? Does it include ages or hometowns? Know the house style of the publications you write for, and you'll boost your query success rates, and endear yourself to editors. "Knowing their house style on things is huge," agrees Karp. "At *Crain's* the first reference is always 'Mr. or Ms. full name as appears on business card, full title, official name of company and location.' It might be something like 'Hoffman Estates, Illinois-based Sears, Roebuck, and Company, Ltd.' They are really huge sticklers for that kind of stuff."

Don't be Afraid to Ask—and Ask Again

If you're new to writing about business—or even if you're not—there may be times when sources use terms or language that you don't understand. Or maybe they're just not making any sense. Pin them down if necessary or ask them to clarify what they're saying. "When you're interviewing business people, do not be afraid to ask them to explain," says Karp. "If you have to ask them five times to explain something, it's not because you're stupid—it's because they're not explaining it very well. Early on, that was a very intimidating aspect for me—talking to someone from a very large company and feeling like I was an idiot because I didn't understand what he was referring to. But oftentimes they just assume that you know things about their sector of business that you don't."

"I think a lot of people are intimidated to call a CEO because their names are names you hear all the time and they are worth billions of dollars," agrees Littman. "It's important to not be intimidated, just like you wouldn't be with any other source. It's sort of a hard thing at first, but once you do it for a while, you meet these guys and you figure out that they're normal."

Use Anecdotes

It's much easier to bring a human perspective to business stories when you can cite examples of people and companies in your articles. "Look for the telling anecdotes," says Rattini. "Business stories very often get weighed down by expert opinions—'this is what an expert thinks business owners should do,' and 'this is how they should do that.' But the anecdotes can speak volumes because they offer specific examples of how one person has put those theories into practice either successfully or not successfully."

Don't be afraid to ask your business sources to back up any claims they make as well. For example, Rattini did many profiles of independent grocery store owners for *IGA Grocergram*, a trade publication. "Just about every single store owner says that he prides himself on customer service. That's great lip service, but I press for specific examples, and those examples usually reveal how they've been able to put that into practice," she says. "Maybe a meat department manager has been packaging meats in smaller packages for his senior citizens or a bakery manager offers free samples every day. Anecdotes again give specific examples of how they've been able to put this into practice and bring a human element into an otherwise disembodied voice of an expert."

For another story on college students and credit card debt, Rattini found a college student who was graduating with a $16,000 credit card balance to his name. "Jason, the student, mentioned that people should think about using debit cards because that helps control their spending," says Rattini. "He gave an example which is something that several other experts had told me, but the fact that he himself had put it into practice made it a stronger recommendation. When you have someone who can tell about his or her own experiences, it gives an extra credibility to it instead of having an expert saying it."

Consider Your Audience

Remember to keep your readers in mind as you write. If you're writing for a trade or business-specific publication, your readers probably have more background in business subjects than if you're writing for a consumer publication aimed at a more general audience. "You assume a different level of knowledge for a consumer than for a trade. With trades, you're pretty much assuming that you're writing for people who work in the industry and they have at least a basic knowledge of operation, standard practices, and terminology," says Rattini. "Be prepared to give a more thorough explanation and perhaps use simpler language and more examples in a consumer magazine than in a trade magazine."

While the editor may dictate the format of the piece, don't be afraid to use a FAQ ("Frequently Asked Questions") or a Q&A format if possible. Both help break complex subjects into simpler, easy-to-understand chunks, says Rattini. For longer stories, you can use sidebars to include relevant terminology or resources for more information.

Tales From the Front: Ari Tye Radetsky

Ari Tye Radetsky of Denver, Colorado, has been freelancing for 10 years. He used his background in computer consulting to establish himself as a freelancer, writing about technological subjects. While he covers a variety of subjects, business and technology are his primary specialties. He offers this advice for freelancers new to writing about business:

Be accurate in your reporting. Remember that your readers will often know as much—or more than—you do about their particular industry or business, and they'll notice if you make mistakes.

Root out the "PR" talk and jargon. Don't fall into the trap of using terms that may have some meaning in a particular industry but don't have a meaning to the average reader—or don't mean what they say. If a business executive says, "this has a fantastic ROI (return on investment)," nail him down and ask how he's measuring that ROI.

Be careful with your terminology. For example, "markets" and "economies" mean similar things but they are not synonyms. Neither are the words "assets" and "current assets" (the latter term refers to property owned by the business that can be easily converted to cash).

Double-check any information you get off the internet. Even if you find it on the website of a major corporation, you should always follow up with the company's PR department to confirm it. The person may have more recent data for you, and your editors will appreciate it when it comes to fact-checking.

Develop multiple story ideas to maximize your research time. For example, you might write about copy-protected CDs from the business side of it, from the technology side, and from the recording industry side. It usually takes little time to spin more than one story out of the same basic research.

Practical Pitching:
Tips for Getting your First (or Fifteenth) Assignment

When pitching a business or personal finance story, your query should include the following elements:

■ An attention-getting lead, with a time peg if possible
■ Enough information about the topic so that the editor knows why her readers will be interested—such as how this will impact their business or their checkbook
■ Details about how you will approach the story
■ An ISG that explains why you're qualified to write the piece

For an example, look at the following query, which sold to *Pages*, a magazine about books. At first glance, you might not think of this is as a business pitch, but it is—it's actually about the business of selling books. While *Pages* usually runs stories about authors and books, I knew this topic would interest readers, and my editor agreed.

I had met John at a recent conference, so I open with a friendly reminder of who I am. While the lead isn't stellar, I think it does catch your attention—it also shows that I've done some background research on the subject. The next paragraph provides more information about the subject, and explains how I'll approach the piece. And the final full paragraph, my ISG, could have been stronger (in fact, I had recently sold my first book—why didn't I mention that?) but notice that I let him know I'd covered writing-related subjects before. If I wrote this query today, I'd pump up this query with my recent personal experience.

Dear John:

It was a real pleasure meeting you in Chicago, and I hope you enjoyed your visit with your parents. I'm writing to follow up on one of the ideas I pitched during our One-on-One:

You've written your first book—a novel, perhaps, or a work of nonfiction. In search of a potential publisher, you pore through books like Writers Market to find the perfect one. Sure, there are hundreds of publishers listed, but did you realize that many of the apparently different houses and imprints may actually be subsidiaries of the same corporation? In fact, according to Guerrilla Marketing for Writers, six conglomerates currently dominate English-language publishing: AOL Time Warner; Bertalsmann; Rupert Murdoch's News Corporation; Pearson, Penquin; Viacom; and Dieter Von Hotlzbrinck.

Does the move toward conglomeration in the publishing industry mean good news or bad news for first-time authors? Are there fewer chances for success with the larger houses or are smaller houses picking up the slack? And how does this affect how authors pitch and present their work? "Under the Umbrella: What Mega-Publishers Mean for First-time Authors" will look at this trend and report on how it affects authors and what changes writers may expect in the future. I'll interview publishing industry experts including editors and agents for the story; while I estimate 1500 words for the piece, that's flexible depending on your needs.

John, are you interested in this topic as a feature for Pages? As you know, I'm a fulltime freelancer who has written for more than 40 national magazines including The Writer, Writer's Digest, Redbook, Marie Claire, Woman's Day, Self, Shape, Parents, Fitness, E-merging Business, and Chamber Executive. As I mentioned, I was originally a lawyer (ugh!) but now write mostly health, fitness, diet/nutrition, bridal/relationships, and writing-related articles; clips are enclosed.

Let me know if you have any questions about this idea or have other pieces I might be right for; otherwise, I'll follow up on this query in a couple of weeks.

Have a great August!

Best,
Kelly James-Enger

The Markets: Where to Sell Business Writing

Business writers have a broad range of markets to choose from, and rates vary depending on the size of the market. While trade magazines tend to pay less than consumer publications, they often provide a steady source of work for freelancers. Some of the biggest markets for business-related writing and their areas of interest include:

General interest magazines—broad range of coverage including business strategies, the economy, personal finance and investing, business profiles, and other related areas.

Business and personal finance magazines—these magazines cover all aspects of business, industry, commerce, and/or personal finance.

Professional and trade journals—depending on the journal, may have a narrower range of interest; many trade magazines cover specific industries or businesses.

Women's and men's magazines—these magazines cover a broad range of subjects including personal finance and topics like saving for college and retirement, investing, buying a home or car, and the like.

"In-flight" magazines—these publications are published by airlines for travelers to read and usually focus on business subjects.

Business-oriented web sites—these markets cover a variety of business topics. As with other online publications, stories tend to run shorter than in print markets and include quizzes, links to other sites and other interactive features.

National/major newspapers—cover all aspects of business and industry.

Regional/city magazines and newspapers—like their national counterparts, regional and city publications also cover a broad range of business-related topics, many with a local angle.

Other Useful Stuff

If you choose to specialize in business writing, you may want to start by focusing on a particular trade, industry or niche. Developing a Rolodex of experts, analysts and other professionals will help you research and report stories accurately. Possible story sources are listed below:

Online resources

Bloomberg.com, www.bloomberg.com. Breaking news from Bloomberg, an information services, news and media company.

Business Week online, www.businessweek.com. Online version of the publication.

Nasdaq Stock Market, www.nasdaq.com. Detailed market information from Nasdaq.

Newsdesk, www.newsdesk.com. Newsdesk offers free email newsletters on business and other topics.

Newswise, www.newswise.com. Newswise offers free email newsletters on business, maintains press releases and an online directory of experts.

New York Stock Exchange online, www.nyse.com. News, current data and other information.

The New York Times online, www.nytimes.com. Online version of the publication.

Profnet, profnet.prnewswire.com/. Search the online database or submit a query to find experts in particular areas; you must be a published freelancer and register to use the service.

Reuters, www.reuters.com. Business information and breaking news.

Wall Street Journal online, www.wsj.com. Online version of the publication.

Governmental agencies, associations and organizations

Commerce Department
14th Street and Constitution Ave., N.W. #5854
Washington, D.C. 20230
Phone: 202-482-2112 Press: 202-482-2741
www.commerce.gov

The Commerce Department acts as a principal advisor to the U.S. president on federal policy affecting industry and commerce. It promotes economic growth, trade and technological development, and provides economic statistics, research and analysis. Staff also answers questions about commerce and business.

Small Business Administration
409 3rd St., S.W. #7000
Washington, D.C. 20416
Phone: 202-205-6605 or 800-827-5722 Press: 202-205-6740
www.sba.gov

The SBA is the U.S. government's principal advocate of small business interests through financial, investment, procurement and management assistance and counseling.

Treasury Department

1500 Pennsylvania Ave., N.W. #3330
Washington, D.C. 20220
Phone: 202-622-1100 Information 202-622-1260
www.ustreas.gov

The Treasury Department formulates and recommends domestic and international financial, economic, tax and broad fiscal policies.

Other Associations/Organizations

American Advertising Federation

1101 Vermont Avenue, NW Suite 500
Washington, D.C. 20005-6306
Phone: 202-898-0089
www.aaf.org

This 50,000-member organization works to advance the business of advertising.

American Bankers Association

1120 Connecticut Ave., N.W.
Washington, D.C. 20036
Phone: 202-663-5000 or 800-BANKERS
www.aba.com

This organization includes primarily commercial banks and trust companies, and represents the more than 2 million Americans who work in banks.

American Finance Association

University of California Berkeley
Hass School of Business
545 Student Services Building
Berkeley, CA 94720-1900
Phone: 800-835-6770
www.afajof.org

The AFA has 8,000 members and consists of college and university professors of economics and finance, bankers, treasurers, analysts, financiers, and others interested in financial problems.

American Institute of Certified Public Accountants
1211 Avenue of the Americas
New York, N.Y. 10036-8775
Phone: 212-596-6200
www.aicpa.org
This is the professional society of accountants who are certified by U.S. states and territories; includes more than 336,000 members.

America's Community Bankers
900 19th St. N.W. Suite 400
Washington, D.C. 20006
Phone: 202-857-3100
www.acbankers.org
This 2,100-member organization consists of savings and loan associations, savings banks, cooperative banks, and savings and loan associations in all U.S. states and territories.

Chamber of Commerce of the United States
1615 H St. NW
Washington, DC 20062
Phone: 202-659-6000
www.uschamber.com
The chamber is a national federation of 3 million business organizations and companies; it maintains a speakers' bureau, compiles statistics and conducts research programs.

Council of Better Business Bureaus
4200 Wilson Boulevard, Suite 800
Arlington, VA 22203-1838
Phone: 703-276-0100
www.bbb.org, www.bbbonline.org
The council is supported by more than 130 local bureaus; it monitors truth and accuracy of national advertising claims, develops information on national charitable organizations, provides information to consumers, and settles consumer complaints through arbitration and other means.

Credit Union National Association
5710 Mineral Point Rd.
Madison, WI 53705-4454
Phone: 800-356-9655
www.cuna.org

This 10,000-member organization serves more than 90 percent of credit unions in the U.S.

Financial Planning Association
4100 E. Mississippi Ave. Suite 400
Denver, CO 80246-3053
Phone: 800-322-4237
www.fpanet.org

This organization has 30,000 members and is made up of individuals involved in the financial planning aspect of the financial planning industry.

National Association of Manufacturers
1331 Pennsylvania Ave. N.W. Suite 600
Washington, D.C. 20004
Phone: 202-637-3000 or 800-814-8468
www.nam.org

The NAM represents the manufacturing industries' views on national and international problems to government; affiliated with 150 local and state trade associations of manufacturers.

National Retail Federation
325 7th St. N.W. Suite 1100
Washington, D.C. 20004
Phone: 202-783-7971 or 800-NRF-HOW2
www.nrf.com

The National Retail Federation represents 50 state retail associations, several dozen national retail associations, and large and small corporate members of the retail industry.

Writers' Organizations and Other Resources

American Society of Business Publication Editors

214 N. Hale Street
Wheaton, IL 60187
Phone: 630-510-4588
www.asbpe.org/
This 700-member organization includes both writers and editors of business, trade and technical publications.

Society of American Business Editors and Writers

c/o University of Missouri, School of Journalism
134 Neff Annex
Columbia, MO 65211-1200
Phone: 573-882-7862
www.sabew.org
This 3,200-member organization consists of active business, economic and financial news writers and editors; also includes business and journalism professors.

Books

Covering Business: A Guide to Aggressively Reporting on Commerce and Building a Powerful Business Beat, by Robert Reed and Glenn Lewin (Marion Street Press, 2005). Aimed at newspaper writers and editors, but jammed full of information on researching corporations, interviewing executives, etc. that would be useful for any business writer.

Math Tools for Journalists, by Kathleen Wickham (Marion Street Press, 2003). An easy-to-use guide to basic math — including business math — all written from the journalists' perspective.

Understanding Financial Statements: A Journalist's Guide, by Jay Taparia (Marion Street Press, 2004). A thorough guide to digging out the details from a company's financial statements, with a focus on unearthing news the companies don't want public.

Calling all Web-Heads:
Writing About Technology

New developments in technology have changed the way we work, the way we play and the way we live—as well as producing a huge demand for freelancers who can report and write on technology-based subjects. As technology's influence continues, so will the need for savvy tech writers. Even the dot-com crashes at the onset of the millennium haven't eliminated the market—technology is still making a major impact on our daily lives and will continue to be a hot beat for writers who can cover it.

While it is a specialized field that requires some working knowledge of technical issues, you needn't be a network administrator to pitch and write articles aimed at business owners or consumers. The key to turning your interest in technology into high-paying assignments is having an understanding of how technology works and being able to communicate sometimes complicated concepts in simple language.

Technology writers often have a background in the field, but it doesn't matter whether that background came about through work or a personal interest in gigabytes and googling. The more important question is whether you can explain technology in easy-to-understand terms, and be able to report stories beyond your personal experience.

Stuck for ideas? Think of the various ways technology impacts your daily life. For example, even I (a complete technophobe) could pitch the following stories:

■ A rundown on the new iPods and other digital music carriers available, comparing their capacity and price, for a fitness magazine

■ A story for a parenting magazine on "Nanny-cams," and how to install one

■ A piece for a local publication on geocaching and places to try this new sport

■ A short piece for a woman's magazine on tips to prevent becoming the victim of identity theft

■ A story for a college publication on how universities are cracking down on students who plagiarize from online sources

My recent life experience could be used in my ISG for all of the above queries, and then I'd call on true experts to research and write the piece. If you're ready to cover tech, read on.

Nuts and Bolts: How to Write About Technology

Start With a Non-Tech Audience
First off, there are plenty of markets that cover technology today. "Computer use is so prevalent today and it's ageless and without gender, so markets everywhere are covering technology," says freelancer and computer consultant Helen Gallagher of Glenview, Illinois, owner of Computer Clarity and author of *Computer Ease* (Virtual Book Worm 2005). "Take *AARP* magazine, which covers technology all the time when they're telling seniors about the benefits of blogging or being online. Airline magazines have articles on how to take your digital photos everywhere you go. Medical magazines in doctors' offices have articles on how to surf online and which search engines to use to find medical information on the web."

If you don't have tech clips, Gallagher suggests approaching nontech magazines with ideas for their readers. The shorter "front-of-the-book" sections of magazines are good places for new writers to break in. "Offer to do a basic piece on dealing with e-mail clutter, the bad effects of multi-tasking, or internet overload," she says. "All of those things are ripe for anybody in the non-tech market. The key is to write about technology but to remember that the audience is non-technical, which I call tech for a lay audience."

You Needn't Be a Geek
While having some background in technology doesn't hurt, you

needn't be a techie whiz to create a specialty in this area. Ask Monique Cuvelier, a freelancer in Boston, who has been writing about technology for more than 12 years. "I think I was just one of the early people who didn't think technology was dorky, and I wasn't afraid to write about it, so I got some interesting stories placed," says Cuvelier. "It seemed like a logical outgrowth from the business writing I'd been doing. Maybe that's the key—for people not to have the idea that you have to wear tape on your glasses or know how to program COBOL before you write something about technology."

Still, though, it helps to have some knowledge of what you're writing about. "For example, I have no idea how to build a data warehousing system, but I know what it's supposed to do when it's built," says Cuvelier. The ability to learn about technology is also important as is the ability to understand how the concepts you're writing about relate to the real world. "You do have to have some foundation and some understanding of technology to write about it," says Sam Greengard, a freelancer who writes about technology and business in West Linn, Oregon. "But you don't have to be a technical expert. I'm a tech generalist, so I try to have a broad knowledge base and then use the analysts and experts and people like that to drill down."

Consider the Impact

Think of technology as a tool. Many people don't care about technology itself, but they do care about its impact on their lives and businesses. When writing about technology you need to think beyond how something functions and explain to readers how this will affect their lives. "Don't try to explain how everything works unless it's a technical pub where you need to do that," says Greengard. "It's better to humanize the story. Don't write about the technology—write about how it helps somebody or how it makes their life better.

"For example, you can't expect to write an article about personal digital assistants ("PDAs"), and explain how they work," says Greengard. "But what you can write about is what are their benefits, what are their problems, and should someone out there buy one—and if they already have one, how can they use it them more effectively."

One of the most effective ways to enliven a technological story is by using some real-people or real-company examples. "Try to include case studies and anecdotes like in any other writing," says Greengard. "I think sometimes those case studies can tell more in a paragraph than a thousand words of explaining it because it's someone really doing it."

Avoid Jargon

Just because you're writing about technology doesn't mean your stories should be dry, technical and laced with jargon. "Editors usually want a conversational tone and something that is easily understood and easily read," says Greengard. "That means boiling it down to simpler terms. You have to avoid acronyms and jargon and passive voice. When a story gets bogged down in jargon and acronyms and this, that and the other thing, it becomes too vague and dense."

The catch-22 is that you don't want to treat the readers like they're morons, either. "There's a fine line when writing about technology. On one hand, often the readers know a lot more than you do, and you have to know what kind of obvious information not to include," says Cuvelier. "But on the other hand, you have to know how to explain complicated systems in plain English—which is harder than it sounds. Too many tech articles sound like they're written for 5-year-olds. You have to tell readers how something works without talking down to them."

Go to the Source(s)

When you're writing about technology, you'll want to develop your own Rolodex of experts to call upon. Possible sources include analysts, professors, engineers, software developers, and Webmasters. But while they may have access to information that you don't, remember that sources are likely to have their own agendas as well. If a software developer praises its latest product, ask for references of "real people" who are already using it. (Just keep in mind that a vendor is usually going to provide you with the names of people who will speak glowingly about their products, so you may have to look for other independent sources as well.) In short, do rely on experts for up-to-date information, but don't take what they—or the people they send you to—say at face value.

Sometimes the most difficult part of a technology story is finding real-life examples to include. Local chambers of commerce and PR companies can often provide leads for possible sources, which can save writers time when they're facing a tight deadline. "I have a stable of PR contacts who I could trust," says Lain Ehmann, a freelancer in Monte Sereno, California who specialized in technology writing before branching out to general business topics. "If I'm looking for someone who, say, can talk about systems integration and the PR agency has referred a legitimate company that wasn't going to make me look bad in the past, I'll check with them to find sources."

Nail Them Down

Even if you have a background in technology, expect to ask questions—and more questions—of the experts you interview. If you don't understand what an engineer or software developer is telling you, you won't be able to effectively explain it to readers later. "Don't let the technical people like engineers get away with some off-the-cuff answer that you don't understand," says Ehmann. "They're usually very accommodating if you say, 'can you explain that again?' or 'what do you mean by that?'"

Accept that you probably won't understand every concept the first time it's explained to you and don't worry about looking stupid. "Never be afraid to ask the 'stupid' questions," says Ehmann. "I think the temptation is to avoid asking the questions because you don't want to sound like an idiot. But the only way you sound like an idiot if you don't ask the questions and you write about it and get something wrong—and then your audience knows that you blew it."

Follow the Trends

In technology, trends come and go very quickly. It can be tough to stay current because the field changes so quickly. If you develop a niche within technology—whether it's covering distance learning, e-commerce, or wireless communication, for example, it helps you keep up-to-date without being overwhelmed.

Ehmann says she sets herself apart from other technology writers by continuing to seek out new markets and refine her focus as trends come and go. "Within the field of technology, there are many subspecialties just as there are in any other field," says Ehmann. "While I can write about technology in general, mostly I write about the business of technology—meaning marketing, management, et cetera—rather than the technology itself."

Once you have a handle on a particular segment of the tech industry, it's smart to expand into other areas to make yourself more marketable. "What editors want is someone who understands technology in general and can talk to the technical people and interview company representatives and write about the technology for their audience," says Ehmann. Even if your technology expertise is limited to only one area, you can use that as a selling point in your query. "Technology crosses so many different areas from networking to e-commerce to software to hardware to telecommunications," says Ehmann. "Once you have a grounding in the basics, you can cross back and forth amongst those very easily."

Consider the Audience

As with any type of writing, you must keep the audience you're writing for in mind. With consumer markets, the stories tend to be less technical. "For example, if people are sitting on an airplane or they're in their doctor's office reading a magazine article about personal digital assistants, they need to know why it's important to them," says Greengard. "So, I need to connect with the average Joe on the street."

With a business trade magazine, however, the audience is employers, employees or both. "People in the business world and they have very different needs and they want more information although again, not necessarily highly technical information," says Greengard. "But they need more information about how-to, like how to effectively use computers and technology. Again, the bottom line is how does it relate to them, how can it make their work better or easier."

Become a Blogger

To write effectively about technology, you have to keep up on what's happening in the industry. Five years ago, no one had heard of a blog. Today, there are more than 4 million blogs online, and many freelancers are using blogs to showcase their work. This is a great idea for writers who specialize in tech—after all, you're expected to keep up on the latest in the field.

"A blog is basically free, as opposed to maybe a couple hundred a year for a website," says Gallagher. "You can change the content instantly, update it by sending an email, and can invite comments to build a platform…it bears a link back to your web site if you have one, it spurs dialog and helps you build readership for your work…it leads to more exposure for your work, and a place to display clips." Writing for your own blog will also give you experience to write for others (for pay!).

Reading blogs about tech-related subjects can help you keep up with what's happening in the field and produce story ideas. "You have to keep on the current edge, just like the companies have to keep current because there's always the next big thing," says Ehmann. "As a tech writer, you have to keep current so you can write about the next big thing."

Tales From the Front: W. Eric Martin

W. Eric Martin is a freelancer in Concord, Hew Hampshire who writes about a variety of subjects, many of which concern some aspect of technology. While he is now the editor of www.BoardgameNews.com, "the best English site for news about board games," and has cut back on his tech-related work, he offers this advice to journalists who want to cover technology:

Make sure that you're describing the technology accurately. Ask questions about everything even if you think you know what's going on.

If you have any doubts or questions, ask the person interviewed or someone familiar with the technology to review what you've written—they can find mistakes more quickly than you can.

Get hands-on experience. If you can actually use the technology, it helps you describe it more accurately. For example, Martin visited a plant in Rhode Island where laptop computers are recycled, which helped him write a more detailed story about the facility. He also was able to get access to the wireless network security system created for the 2002 Olympics, which gave him a different perspective when it came to writing a piece about it.

Define any jargon or terms the reader may not know. If it's just a word or two, you can address it in the story; otherwise, you may want to include sidebars to explain concepts or how something works. If you're talking about a new technology, describe it in terms of something the readers will be familiar with.

Don't be taken in by hype. There's way too much talk in terms of revolutionizing industries and potential long-term results because of new technology. If you don't know what the effects of a new technology are going to be, don't oversell what you're talking about. Let the experts and people in the field speak for themselves. And instead of having a product's manufacturer or developer predict its usefulness, ask people who actually use it.

Practical Pitching:
Tips for Getting your First (or Fifteenth) Assignment

When pitching a technology story, your query should include the following elements:
- An attention-getting lead, with a time peg if possible
- Enough information about the topic so that the editor knows why her readers will be interested
- Details about how you will approach the story
- An ISG that explains why you're qualified to write the piece

For an example, look at the following query, which sold to *Writer's Digest*. Note how the writer has taken a technology idea (managing email) and customized it for the readers of the magazine—writers who use email every day. She shows that she knows her subject, cites some recent research, and does a great job of showing why she's the perfect candidate for the story. Note, too, how this idea could easily be customized for dozens of other magazines, with little effort on the writer's part.

Dear Robin,

Is your e-mail a time drain?

This idea came as a result of discussions with editors and writers at a conference last weekend. Some close their e-mail program when on deadline. Others are embarrassed by their inability to reply, or regret that a quick check of e-mail turns in to an hour lost and wasted, reading, replying, losing focus, and falling behind on tasks.

Research conducted in London this year, and supported by Pew Research stated that excessive multi-tasking is equivalent to smoking four marijuana cigarettes, in terms of its effect on our concentration.

Our efforts to be productive writers, whether full or part-time, are thwarted by wasted hours we can't recapture, and long hours at the computer with nothing to show for it. Too many writers lose focus because of the continual interruption of e-mail and instant-messaging, yet don't have the confidence and skill needed to manage e-mail as a business tool. This is a basic skill needed in business today.

As both a writer and computer consultant, I will offer solutions to manage e-mail in folders, organize and sort replies by topic, find any e-mail within seconds, and think before clicking "Send." The strategies for professional e-mail management, unfortunately, don't pertain to those who use AOL or MSN as a mail client. This piece would encourage readers to use an e-mail client such as Netscape, Outlook or Outlook Express to enjoy these features.

I'm proposing an 800-word article on the confidence readers will gain by managing e-mail as the professional business tool it is. The reality is we receive no formal training in e-mail etiquette, forwarding, business writing, or time management, but one e-mail error can ruin our chances with an editor or cause us to miss a coveted assignment.

To refresh your memory, in addition to contributing to Writer's Digest, I've contributed over 100 articles to trade and consumer magazines, and write business and technology articles for readers at all levels. My clients include Lifestyle Media, PAGES, and Training Media Review in Cambridge, Massachusetts. It would be my pleasure to contribute this story for you.

Best regards,
Helen Gallagher

The Markets: Where to Sell Technology Writing

You may be surprised at the range of markets for technology articles. Rates vary depending on the size of the market. Because of technology's continuing impact on business and industry, trade magazines are also a lucrative market for technology writers. Some of the biggest markets for technology-related writing and their areas of interest include:

General interest magazines—broad range of coverage including technology's impact on business and the economy, devices and technologies that make everyday life easier, the latest developments and other related areas.

Technology magazines—these magazines are devoted specifically to technology but have different focuses and audiences; read closely before pitching ideas.

Business magazines—these magazines cover all aspects of technology as it relates to business and industry including how-to, the pros and cons of different technologies, profiles, and the like.

Professional and trade journals—depending on the journal, this may be a narrower range of interest; many trade magazines cover specific industries or businesses.

Women's and men's magazines—these magazines cover technology as it relates to daily life, personal finance, recreation, parenting, and other subjects.

Business-oriented web sites—these markets cover a variety of technology topics, again focusing on how they affect business and industry. As with other online publications, stories tend to run shorter than in print markets and include quizzes, links to other sites and other interactive features.

National/major newspapers—cover all aspects of technology and its implications for business and individuals.

Regional/city magazines and newspapers—like their national counterparts, regional and city publications also cover a broad range of technology-related subjects, many with a local angle.

Other Useful Stuff

Because technology changes so quickly, many writers rely on websites, email newsletters, blogs, and other online sources to keep tabs on what's happening. Technology writers often must interview consultants, analysts, and other experts, and may find the following sources helpful.

Web Resources

Bloomberg.com, www.bloomberg.com. Breaking news from Bloomberg, an information services, news and media company.

Business Week online, www.businessweek.com. Online version of the publication.

CNET.com, www.CNET.com. Site that includes IT information and news; includes free newsletters.

Free Tech Mail, www.freetechmail.org. The site lists hundreds of free IT newsletters available online.

Hoover's Online , www.hoovers.com. Business and financial news from Hoover's, a business consulting company.

IDG.net, www.IDG.net. Comprehensive site that also includes free email newsletters.

Information Technology Professional's Resource Center, www.itprc.com. This site lists online data networking resources.

InformationWeek.com, www.informationweek.com. Online component of *Information Week* magazine.

IT papers.com, www.ITpapers.com. Site includes thousands of articles on IT subjects for reference.

The New York Times online, www.nytimes.com. Online version of the publication.

Pew Internet and American Life Project, www.pewinternet.org. Information about how the internet affects American families; great place for story ideas.

Profnet, profnet.prnewswire.com. Search the online database or submit a query to find experts in particular areas; you must be a published freelancer and register to use the services.

www.techtarget.com, whatis.techtarget.com. Online encyclopedia of IT-related terms.

TechWeb, www.techweb.com. Reports on tech news; includes email newsletters and an IT terms encyclopedia.

Wall Street Journal online, www.wsj.com. Online version of the publication.

Wired News, www.wired.com. Online version of *Wired* magazine.

ZDNet, www.zdnet.com. Another source for tech news.

IT Consulting and Advisory Firms

Aberdeen Group, www.aberdeen.com. IT market analysis and consulting firm; provides sources for articles.

AMR Research, www.amrresearch.com. IT market analysis and consulting firm; provides sources for articles.

Forrester Research, www.forrester.com. IT research and consulting firm; provides sources for articles.

Gartner Group, www.gartner.com. IT research and consulting firm; provides analysts and sources for articles.

IDC, www.idc.com. Provider of technology forecasts, insights and advice; provides article sources.

Yankee Group, www.yankeegroup.com. IT research and consulting firm; provides sources for articles.

Other Associations/Organizations

Computing Technology Industry Association
1815 S. Meyers Road, Suite 300
Oakbrook Terrace, IL 60181-5228
Phone: 630.678.8300
www.comptia.org
The association has more than 20,000 companies and professional IT members in the computing and communications markets; serves as an information clearinghouse and industry resource.

Independent Computer Consultants Association
11131 S. Towne Square, Suite F
St. Louis, MO 63123
Phone: 314-892-1675 or 800-774-4222
www.icca.org
The association is a national network of independent computer consultants.

Internet Society
1775 Wiehle Ave., Suite 102
Reston, VA 20190-5108
Phone: 703-326-9880
www.isoc.org
The Internet Society consists of 20,000 technologists, developers, educators, researchers, government representatives, and business people.

US Internet Industry Association

5810 Kingstowne Center Drive
Suite 120, PMB 212
Alexandria, VA 22315-5711
Phone: 703-924-0006
www.usiia.org

This trade association provides members with business news, information and support relating to internet commerce, content and connectivity.

Writers' Organization

Society for Technical Communication

901 N. Stuart St. Suite 904
Arlington, VA 22203-1822
Phone: 703-522-4114
www.stc.org

The 18,000-member society includes writers, editors, educators, scientists, engineers, artists, and publishers who work in field of technical communication.

Books

The Tech Writer's Survival Guide: A Comprehensive Handbook for Aspiring Technical Writers, by Janet Van Wicklen (Checkmark Books, 2001). Although aimed at technical writers, this book has good background information and tips for writing about technological subjects.

Technical Writing for Dummies, by Sheryl Lindsell-Roberts (Hungry Minds, 2001). Also geared for technical writers, but includes useful information including a rundown of punctuation and grammar rules, abbreviations, and an appendix of technical terms.

The Mommy (or Daddy) Track: Writing About Parenting

Up to your ears in dirty diapers and carpools? As a parent, you're uniquely qualified to write for one of the largest freelance markets there is. Hundreds of magazines, newspapers, and websites are constantly in search of parenting pieces that entertain and inspire as they inform. New and inexperienced writers often break into freelancing by writing about parenting issues, and writers who develop a specialty in this area often find that they need look no further than their own families for story ideas.

But writing about parenting and child care is more than simply relating personal experience—parenting writers are expected to keep up on trends, locate and interview experts, and provide plenty of service for readers.

Every time I teach, there are several stay-at-home parents who have realized that freelancing is a great way to make some money from home. Pitching parenting ideas is an excellent way to launch your freelance career, and you can easily transition from covering child care subjects to others as well. Plus, as Janet Mazur noted in chapter two, raising kids practically guarantees you story ideas. And you can bet if you've faced an issue with your children, there are millions of other parents dealing with the same issues.

As a relatively new parent myself, I can tell you I've had dozens of story ideas, many of which involve the age-old question of "how do I get this baby to sleep?" Seriously, as the mother of a toddler, here's a selection of story ideas I'm uniquely qualified to pitch:

■ An article for a parenting magazine on introducing table food to your baby (should you insist on organics, for example?)

■ An article for a fitness magazine rating the plethora of jogging strollers available

■ A piece for a local magazine on indoor family-friendly activities to help you survive the winter months (I've found the local children's museum to be a sanity-saver)

■ A short piece for a food and wine magazine on the increasing number of restaurants that have "childfree" nights

■ A story for a general interest magazine on college savings plans

■ A piece for a woman's magazine on what to consider before you write your will

Wow—with all those ideas, I'd better start querying! Use your children, or those around you, for story ideas, and look for topics that you know other parents face or will face. That's the key for cracking this market.

The Nuts and Bolts: Writing About Parenting and Child Care

Don't Preach

Ask any new parent and he or she will tell you—when it comes to parenting, everyone has an opinion and no one thinks twice about sharing theirs with you (like it or not). If the baby cries, pick her up immediately—or she'll be traumatized. Nope, that's the worst thing you can do—you'll spoil her if you don't let her cry herself to sleep. Let him suck on a pacifier and he'll need thousands of dollars' worth of orthodontia…or take it away from him too early and he'll need therapy for separation anxiety years later.

Complicating matters is that while many of these issues are intensely personal issues, parents face dozens if not hundreds of decisions every day that will affect their children's welfare. What's a mom or dad to do? Most look to parenting or child care publications for advice, information and support.

The most important rule in writing about parenting is to avoid preaching or implying that there is only one way to do something. "Parenting is so subjective. Everyone feels differently about how they want to parent and you don't want to turn people off," says Melanie Bowden, a freelancer in Davis, California, author of *Why Didn't Anyone Tell Me? True Stories of New Motherhood* (Booklocker, 2006). "You want to say 'this is one option.' A typical example is the family bed issue—people get touchy about it and it's really a personal decision. It's the same thing with breastfeeding. When you write about anything like that, you want to give options but also support whatever people decide to do."

Provide Service

When you write about parenting, you're often providing some kind of service to the person reading the article. In fact, "how-to" articles are the most prevalent kind of parenting stories and for good reason.

"Parents are busy and they want you to get to the point," says Kathy Sena, a freelancer in Manhattan Beach, California. "They want practical, real-world tips. They love sidebars, boxes and bullets, and so do parenting magazines. Parents want to hear from experts, and a little theory is fine—but get to the point quickly and show them how they can use what you're telling them."

Find Supporting Experts

OK, so you're a parent. A good parent, possibly even a great parent. But it takes more than that to write with authority about parenting and child care. "Just because you're a parent, don't assume you're an expert on parenting," says Lain Ehmann, a freelancer in Monte Sereno, California. "I think that a lot of people think once they have a kid, it's an easy topic to write about. For that very reason, the people who can write about parenting well stand out that much more clearly."

Even if you have personal experience with an issue, you'll probably need to back up the advice you offer with more authoritative opinions and quotes. "You still need the experts, the research, and the writing skills like in any other field," says Ehmann. That means you may have to interview pediatricians, child development experts, dieticians, or teachers in addition to including real-life anecdotes. And in most cases, you won't want to rely on your child's doctor as an expert—editors prefer someone who is established or well-known in his or her field. Call organizations like the American Medical Association, the American Dietetic Association, or other associations listed in this chapter, and ask for referrals to members who specialize in the area you're writing about.

Write for the Audience

Remember that parents come in all ages, both sexes, and are of every race, ethnicity and religion. This may seem obvious but too often writers simply assume that their family traditions—such as celebrating Christmas—are embraced by all readers. "Unless a magazine has a very specific audience, you're going to have to appeal to a wide range of parents," says Ehmann. "You've got stay-at-home moms, working moms, stay-at-home dads, working dads, two-mother couples, two-father couples, Christian, Jewish, you name it. Parenting cuts across all that, and you have to be mindful of that as you're writing because it's very easy to offend people in the parenting realm."

On the other hand, if you're writing for a publication aimed at a more narrow audience—say, stay-at-home mothers or parents who home-school their children, it's okay to focus your story on that group of people. Just keep the audience in mind as you write the piece.

Consider Regional Publications

While many writers aspire to be published in national parenting magazines like *Child, Parents*, and *Parenting*, there are hundreds of regional parenting and child care publications as well. The vast majority of them need and use freelance material. The rates aren't high but these markets are a good place for new freelancers to get assignments and clips—and offer reprint possibilities as well. Keep in mind, though, that the editors are often overworked and understaffed—and that means slow response times. "When you're talking about small regional publications, you have to be really patient in terms of them getting back to you," says Bowden.

Regional publications may also want you to use local experts and sources for articles; make sure you know what the editor wants before you start the story. "For local publications, look and see what types of stories they run. If they have something they run every year at the same time, offer to write it because the staffers are sick of writing it," suggests Bowden. "For example, some magazines run stories every summer like things to do with your kids, or round-ups of local camps, and people on staff are tired of doing that. It is a grind, but it can get you into the magazine."

Look Beyond Your Own Experience

No doubt that your own children or grandchildren will provide you with fodder for story ideas. But don't neglect articles aimed at other ages as well. While there's a bigger market for stories aimed at parents of infants to school-aged children than for the parents of teenagers, you don't want to pigeonhole yourself by only writing about babies simply because you have a new one at home. "Look beyond your own kids for ideas and anecdotes for your stories," agrees Ehmann. "I can be really narrow-sighted because I have younger kids so I tend to focus on younger kids. Yet the scope of any given publication may be ages 3 to 12, so you need to go beyond your own immediate experiences."

But Don't be Afraid to Share

At the same time, though, your first-hand examples can enrich your writing. Readers may find it easier to relate to someone who's "been there." "I've found that the specific is universal in parenting writing—and probably in all writing," says Sena. "For example, when I wrote about the problems I had with breastfeeding when my son was born, I got into the nitty-gritty details of my specific situation. But I received many e-mails saying things like 'that's exactly what I went through!'"

Your parenting experience is an important part of the equation when it comes to writing about it, and one of the things that can make your ISG a slam-dunk for parenting topics. Don't be afraid to share your own struggles—those kind of relatable anecdotes can make your query stand out from the pack, and net you assignments.

Include Anecdotes

Your personal story is a great place to start. But because there are so many different approaches to parenting, readers like hearing about more than one person's experience or opinion in child care articles. A wide range of sources helps ensure that readers will find something in an article than benefits them.

"Advice varies greatly, especially when it comes to parenting," says Diane Benson Harrington, a freelancer in Madison, Wisconsin. "Since every child is unique, I think it's important to give parents more than one way to solve a problem or look at an issue. I also like to interview more than one expert (I talk to a minimum of three, plus parents themselves, for nearly every story) because I like to make sure the advice is sound. If two or more people sing the same tune, that provides a sounder basis for the idea."

Create New Spins on Evergreen Topics

Many parenting stories cover topics like health, child development, discipline, and nutrition. While these subjects are covered over and over again, look for a new angle or new approach to sell your story idea. "Because it's happening for the first time to you, you think it's a new fresh idea, but that's not always the truth," says Ehmann. "Although parenting publications tend to repeat a lot of the same issues they want a new take on it. For example, just because you're going through the 'should I work/should I stay home?' debate, the publications have probably been through that up, down, sideways, and back and forth, so you need to think of a new spin on it."

Although you may need to come up with a fresh approach, parenting writers have an endless list of "evergreen" story ideas to choose from. Topics like infant first aid, children's health, how to choose a babysitter, how to help kids prepare for and succeed in school, discipline strategies, inexpensive craft activities, proper nutrition, ways to talk to kids about difficult subjects…the list goes on and on. The trick is coming up with a new or unique angle.

"Parenting is a never ending subject," agrees Bowden. "Stories about health and development are popular. Discipline is a big topic, as are helping kids do well in school, socializing, personality traits, dealing with bullies, things like that. Parenting magazines are also really big on seasonal stuff, especially back-to-school issues. They'll run things in October about how to make a Halloween costume, for example, and they're always looking for stuff on Christmas and holidays."

Offer Reprint Rights

Finally, don't overlook reprint possibilities. The issues parents face are pretty similar from East Coast to West, and as a result, parenting articles can offer extra bucks in reprint sales. In fact, many parenting writers maximize their income by selling reprint rights to a variety of regional publications. Melanie Bowden maintains a database of regional publications for this purpose. "Sometimes I'll sell an article to a local publication and then I'll do a huge email to that huge database, offering it as a reprint. You've already written it and it's not much more work except for putting a letter together," she says. "Most small regionals are open to that—they're not that picky because they need content. I get anywhere from $30 to $75 or $80 for a regional reprint." [See chapter 16 for more advice on selling reprints.]

Sena also developed a network of regional publications for her parenting and health stories and resells most of the articles she writes. "About 40 percent of my income comes from reprints," says Sena. "The checks aren't that big—maybe $50 or $75 a story—but they add up quickly!" And even those small checks mean you're getting published, and building your freelance career.

Tales from the Front: Diane Benson Harrington

Diane Benson Harrington has been writing since she was 12 and freelancing fulltime since 1989. Harrington, who lives in Madison, Wisconsin, had already written a few parenting articles before she became a mom herself. She cracked markets like *Parents* and *Parenting* once she had children of her own. She's covered a variety of parenting and child care subjects and teaches online query-writing classes as well, and offers the following tips for writers who want to break into this field:

Do use anecdotes. Nothing makes a story more appealing and easier to relate to than real-life examples of what kids/parents have done or experienced.

Do talk to more than one or two people. You want to corroborate any advice you're providing (because, depending on the topic, the wrong advice could be harmful to a child). Plus, interviewing a well-chosen handful of people makes a story more comprehensive and gives you better information to draw from.

Do use conversational writing. Write like you're talking to a friend so the story will be easy to read. Be sure to use a confident tone, too, so the readers feel confident that this "friend" knows what she's talking about.

Do come up with fresh twists on old topics. Parenting magazines recycle story topics all the time, out of necessity. (Parents always want to read about potty-training, discipline, behavior, education, etc.) For example, instead of an article on general childproofing, Harrington pitched an article called "Childproofing: The Advanced Class," about how parents can get lax on safety issues when their children reach the age of five—and what parents still need to be vigilant about. Instead of a bland article on preparing kids for school, she pitched "What Teachers Wish Parents Knew."

Don't write in long, wordy sentences. Parents are pressed for time. Bullet points and subheadings make for easier, faster reading—and they help you organize your stories.

Don't assume there is only one answer to every problem. The one-size-fits-all approach to parenting is misguided and leaves plenty of readers feeling left out.

Practical Pitching:
Tips for Getting your First (or Fifteenth) Assignment

When pitching a parenting story, your query should include the following elements:

■ An attention-getting lead, often anecdotal in nature
■ Enough information about the topic so that the editor knows why parents will be interested in and impacted by the story
■ Details about how you will approach the piece, including the types of sources you plan to interview
■ An ISG that explains why you're qualified to write the piece

For an example, look at the following query, which sold to *Parenting*. The writer has written a lead that includes a personal anecdote, and described why parents will be interested in her subject matter. She's clear about the length and approach of the story, and the type of sources she will include. And note her ISG—it's a slam-dunk. Once again, this is an idea just about any parent could pitch, but the writer's light, upbeat tone and practical approach to the subject guarantee a sale.

Dear Sarah:

Grandparents may be the only group of people who love speaking to very young children on the telephone. It requires a deep level of patience that many parents find hard to muster. While supervised phone chatting at an early age can be fun, when is it acceptable for a child to begin answering incoming calls solo? (For example, when I call my friend, her three-year-old daughter who has a speech impediment beats her to the phone every time. I don't find it a charming five-minute interlude, but a total annoyance.)

My five-year-olds never pick up the phone. I've not encouraged them, and it has never occurred to them to do so. But is now the time to begin coaching them? When is the right time for kids to start answering the phone? Is it considered rude to let your kids answer, or rude not to, since it is a necessary part of learning how to do it properly? Is there a better age to start than others? What about outgoing calls? Should it be for emergency only, with every kid who can punch a button knowing how to dial 911?

Are you interested in a piece for your Ages and Stages: 5 to 7 years section called "Calling All Telephone Trainees"? For this 300-word article, I'll speak to a parent to find out the telephone rules in their home (or maybe a funny story about it), as well as a child development expert for advice on how to handle incoming and outgoing calls.

I've been a part-time freelancer for nearly three years and full-time mom of 6-year-old triplets, specializing in parenting topics. I'm a contributing writer with Chicago Parent magazine and my articles have also appeared in Parenting and The Christian Science Monitor. In addition, I'm surrounded by children of all ages daily (sometimes willingly), whether volunteering at school or hosting play dates. Before becoming a mom, I managed corporate marketing communications programs.

Do you think your readers will enjoy this article?

Sincerely,
Jill S. Browning

The Markets: Where to Sell your Work

Many of the smaller and regional markets for parenting articles may not be listed in publications like *Writer's Digest*. While national magazines pay more than $1/word and up for parenting articles, regional markets, web sites, and newspapers offer varying rates.

Some of the biggest markets for parenting-related writing include:

National parenting magazines—these glossy markets cover nearly every aspect of parenting and child care including children's health, nutrition, development, childhood diseases, first aid, and preventive medicine; rates are high, but can be difficult to break into.

Regional parenting magazines and publications—many writers start with these publications as there is less competition than at the national glossies. Coverage area depends on the publication but many focus on local events, activities, and resources.

Women's and men's magazines—these magazines, particularly women's publications, often include parenting and child care subjects either in a regular section of the magazine or as features. Stories range from typical service pieces to features to essays to travel topics.

General interest magazines—the markets may cover trends in parenting, new research, children's health, and other related topics.

Parenting-oriented web sites—these markets cover a variety of child care topics. As with other online publications, stories tend to run shorter than in print markets and include quizzes, links to other sites and other interactive features.

National/major newspapers—cover parenting and family issues; often have a section devoted to family life.

Regional/city general interest magazines and newspapers—like their national counterparts, regional and city publications also often include parenting and child care subjects.

Other Useful Stuff

Often when you're writing about parenting, you'll have to find qualified experts. Some possible sources are given below, along with other associations that may be helpful:

Associations/Organizations

American Academy of Pediatrics
141 Northwest Point Boulevard
Elk Grove Village, IL 60007-1098
Phone: 847-434-4000
www.aap.org
This 60,000-member organization consists of pediatricians.

American Dietetic Association

216 W. Jackson Boulevard
Chicago, IL 60606-6995
Phone: 312-899-0040
eatright.org

This 64,000-member organization includes registered dietitians and other dietetic professionals.

American Medical Association

515 N. State St.
Chicago, IL 60610
Phone: 312-464-5000
www.ama-assn.org

The AMA is the largest medical organization in the country, consisting of 297,000 medical doctors.

American Pediatric Society & Society for Pediatric Research

3400 Research Forest Drive, Suite B7
The Woodlands, TX 77381-4259
Phone: 281-419-0052
www.aps-spr.org

The society includes M.D. educators and researchers interested in the study of childhood diseases, prevention of illness and promotion of children's health.

National PTA/National Congress of Parents and Teachers

330 N. Wabash Ave., Suite 2100
Chicago, IL 60610-3690
Phone: 312-670-6782 or 800-307-4PTA
www.pta.org

This 6,500,000-member organization consists of parents, teachers, students, principals and administrators.

Parents Helping Parents (PHP)

3041 Olcott St.
Santa Clara, CA 95054-3222
Phone: 408-727-5775
Website: www.php.com

This organization helps special-needs children receive care, services, education and acceptance.

Parents Without Partners
1650 S. Dixie Highway, Suite 510
Boca Raton, FL 33432
Phone: 561-391-8833 or 800-637-7974
www.parentswithoutpartners.org
This organization aims to alleviate the problems of single parents relating to their kids.

Other Resources for Writers

Parenting Publications of America
5820 Wilshire Blvd, Suite 500
Los Angeles, CA 90036-4500
Phone: 323-937-5514
www.parentingpublications.org
Consisting of mostly regional parenting publications, this organization promotes publications for and about parents and compiles statistics. PPS is also a source for possible reprint markets as well.

Taking a Trip: Writing About Travel

There's an ongoing interest in travel whether it's to local, inexpensive family attractions or high-budget adventures to the other side of the world. While well-paid fulltime travel journalists are somewhat rare, there are many markets for the writer who wants to include travel stories among his or her repertoire. How do travel writers turn their vacations into high paying article assignments? What kinds of markets are interested in travel stories? How you can break into this popular area? Read on to learn how you can turn your travels—whether they're close to home or thousands of miles away—into an income-producing sideline.

Keep in mind, though, that travel writing is a crowded field. In addition to the handful of pros—people who specialize solely in travel and make their living from it—there and thousands more writers who will do a travel story here and there. To break into the field, you need to come up with more than a tried-and-true travel idea. As a new freelancer, study the market and try to come up with and idea or approach that editors haven't thought of before.

Let's use Chicago as an example—I live 20 miles west of the city, and let's say I want to pitch some Chicago-related travel pieces. Here are a few examples I thought of off the top of my head:

■ A round-up on local museums with kid-friendly exhibits for a parenting magazine

■ A story on great places to run in Chicago for a running or fitness magazine

■ A story on the local breweries Chicago is becoming known for aimed at a food and wine magazine

■ A rundown on the best Cubs, Sox, Bulls, and Bears bars in the city for a sports magazine

■ A story covering and rating the outlet malls that pepper the edges of the Chicago suburbs for a local magazine

You probably know more about your hometown that you realize, and if don't mind keeping track of details, why not pitch a few travel stories as well? Start with small or regional publications to build some clips; national travel magazines are hard to crack unless you have a background in travel writing.

Breaking In

As I mentioned, travel writing can be a difficult specialty to get into, in part because so many journalists—both new and experienced—want to enter the field. (Isn't it obvious why? Write about travel and you can start writing off your trips and vacations—as business expenses! What could be better?) While some travel writers start out as freelancers writing about travel, most get into this area after they've already established themselves in another specialty. Using your current contacts to nail your first travel writing assignments is one of the easiest ways to get your foot in the door—that's how Leslie Gilbert Elman of Manhattan, New York got her first travel piece.

"I had been writing women's service features for a magazine that also ran travel stories," says Elman. "The editor and I had a solid, long-standing relationship. One month, she needed someone to write a travel piece and she assigned it to me. It was something of a perk, since she knew and liked me. That gave me my first bona fide 'destination' story."

But afterwards, Elman found it difficult to obtain additional assignments. She decided to write some pieces for newspapers on spec to obtain clips and build her portfolio. "One of them sold to the *Dallas Morning News*. In a way, that sale was the most satisfying because it was made on a totally blind query," says Elman, who's also the author of *The Ladies' Room Reader Quiz Book* (Conari Press, 2004). "The travel editor wasn't someone I knew. She didn't have to buy the piece, but she did. That gave me confidence."

Be Ready to Work

Perhaps no other non-fiction writing field produces such a glamorous image as travel writing. Travel writers loll about on pristine white beaches, an exotic rum drink in one hand as they jot a few notes about their luxurious all-expenses-paid trip for a thousand-dollar payoff. Yeah, right. Ask any travel writer, and she'll tell you the reality is far removed from this idyllic image.

"Travel writing is not a vacation. If you're doing it right, you're working hard day and night," says Elman. "You're interviewing all sorts of people, from hotel managers to locals in the markets. You're shooting photos, taking notes and juggling a million ideas at any given time." If the idea of having to "work" during your vacation turns you off, then this field may not be right for you.

"It's easy to abuse the privilege of being a travel writer. There are a lot of poseurs who enter the field thinking that it's a lark," says Elman. "Those people don't last long. Professionals in the industry—writers, editors, and PR people—talk to each other. You have to comport yourself as a professional and maintain a good reputation or you won't make it."

Don't Quit Your Day Job—Yet

Unlike some other writing specialties—like health, business and technology—it's more difficult to make a good living only writing travel stories. As a result, most writers cover other areas in addition to travel. "Travel writing is highly competitive," says Elman. "It is very hard to sell stories and establish relationships with reputable publications. It's really not an area for beginners."

Many travel writers have developed complementary specialties. They may write about travel and business, for example, or travel and food, or travel and sports. "I've never just gone and done a travel story," says Tim Harper, a freelancer in Ridgewood, New Jersey who's written dozens of travel articles. "What I've done is tied together travel stories with other stories. Let's say a magazine sends me someplace to do a feature. I'll try to bring them more than they asked me to do. I'll come back and say, 'you sent me to Sweden to do this business story on the Swedish economy but I also have this nice little travel story on Sweden in winter—would you like that?' A lot of times they'll buy it," says Harper. "But if not, I've offered it to them and can then sell it elsewhere."

And most journalists wind up covering more than one story on trips to maximize their income. "You don't go for one article—you can't," says freelancer Tom Brosnahan of Concord, Massachusetts, who's authored more than 35 books on travel and now runs several successful travel websites, including www.TurkeyTravelPlanner.com, www.stMoritz TravelPlanner.com, and www.NewEnglandTravelPlanner.com.

"You can repurpose the material," agrees JoAnn Milivojevic, a freelancer in Chicago who has specialized in travel and now writes travel articles in addition to working as a certified Pilates instructor. "It's more fun, too. I try to think of how many ways I can slice and dice the information and who would be interested in it."

The Ethics of Writing Travel

One of the hottest issues facing travel writers is the question of whether to accept "comps," or complimentary trips. Writers and editors may be invited to all-expenses-paid, fact-finding trips sponsored by local or national tourist offices, tour organizers, resorts, airlines or other companies. Some publications prohibit travel writers from accepting this kind of "subsidized" travel because editors believe they can influence a writer's objectivity.

Should you accept comps? The bottom line is that it may be impossible to make a living writing travel if you don't, say many experienced travel writers.

Know Your Subject

With other types of writing—say parenting or health—you can usually research a story through telephone interviews and by reading background material, studies, and the like. With travel, there's simply no substitute for knowing the destination you're covering, whether you're writing a guidebook or a service-related travel story. "If you really know what you're talking about, the reader can sense the depth that comes through," says Brosnahan. "You want a sense of background in your writing."

You can provide this sense of background by including concrete details—like converting the price of a cheap dinner to American dollars. When you're traveling, make notes of your surroundings so that you can incorporate them later on. And don't just rely on your eyes—use all five senses. What does the market smell like? What sounds do you hear as you wake up in the morning? What flavors does the local cuisine feature? Keeping a travel diary will help you recall these kinds of specifics.

"It's really what you see, what you smell, what you hear, and what you taste that sets the place apart," says Milivojevic. "And have conversations with people. It's really important to talk to everyone from the cab driver and the store owner to the other higher officials you might have access to. Talking to the guy or gal on the corner—that's how you find out what a place is really like."

Think Service

A few travel stories simply tell a story about a person's journey. When writing service-related travel articles, though, you want to deliver as much relevant information about the destination. That doesn't mean your stories should read like business memos or be limited to a list of phone numbers, prices, and travel tips. Find your voice and write creatively, and you'll be more likely to sell your work. "For magazine writing to be successful, you have to try to get 110 percent into the article," says Brosnahan. "All the service stuff, plus enough of your personality to really build your reputation. That is what is going to differentiate you from other writers—you have to be kind of stylish."

You usually should put something of yourself into the story. "Write about something you've done. The stuff that looks and sounds bad is where you've gotten it from secondary sources. What people want to read about mostly now is the story, and generally that's your story," says Harper. "For example, my story on narrow boating in England opened with my son falling in the water. That really got us into the whole experience of it, and what it was like to be on this boat and mooring and having lunch in the canal side pubs, which were very unique in their own way. Do something a little different. Think of travel editors as movie critics. They've seen a lot of bad stuff and they tend to like anything a little different."

Take Photos

While it depends on the market, one of the most effective ways to increase your travel-writing sales is by including photographs with your stories. "Certainly for newspaper, when you can send them a complete package, you're more likely to make the sale," says Milivojevic. "It makes the editor's life easier and any time you can save them the hassle, you're a better candidate in their minds."

Agreeing to provide photos with travel stories also improves your bottom line—markets will pay additional for photos, and you may make more on the photos than the story itself! If you're an inexperienced photographer, take a class to learn the basics of photography including what types of film work best in different situations and how to frame shots. Check with the markets to learn how they want photos submitted—most now expect you to have digital shots that can easily be emailed. Forget those cheap plastic throw-away cameras you can pick up at the drug store. A good digital camera is worth the expense, particularly if you want to make travel writing one of your main specialties.

Gather the Information

Remember that readers are going to rely on and use the information you provide them, so it must be accurate. Double-check data like names, addresses, phone numbers, rates, dates of events, and other relevant information before you turn in the story. When traveling or researching a story, keep detailed files of any information that you may want to use in the future. Most travel writers come home with sheaths of papers, contacts, notes, and other background that they can then use in the future.

"I'll often take one of those accordion binders with me and separate it into sections for restaurants, lodging, and attractions," says Milivojevic. "Then I grab brochures and magazines and stuff like that and just stuff them into the proper categories. When I get home, everything is there." Monica Bhide, who covers travel subjects in addition to food writing, takes an extra shoulder bag on every trip and brings it home loaded with background on the locales she's seen.

Consider the Markets

When writing travel, consider the markets before you pitch articles. Is the magazine aimed at an affluent audience? Is the focus adventure travel or more sedate trips? Targeting your queries will help you get more assignments and spin more than one story out of every trip you take.

"I think that's part of the pitching process. I've gathered all the research and have it all on a plate. Then I look at who my audience is for this material and what they want to know, and then what audience does a particular magazine serve," says Milivojevic. "So, for example for a family-oriented magazine, I'm going to want to tell them about the family oriented activities on the Cayman Islands and maybe interview a kid or two while I'm at the Turtle Farm. If I'm doing a nightlife story for another magazine, that's going to be a completely different spiel, it's going to be sexier, and more sensual. It's going to be set at night, and be more about the music and cocktails, and that kind of thing."

Look beyond the "typical" markets when pitching travel stories, too. "A travel writer can sell stories to the resort market, regional city magazines, newspapers, business publications and even political newspapers," says freelancer Jackie Dishner of Phoenix, Arizona, who writes about travel, arts and entertainment. "You can write travelogues (narratives about your trip), destination pieces (features that tell the reader where to go when visiting some place), shopping stories, food pieces, etc. I write shopping stories for one magazine on a regular basis, I write destination pieces occasionally for a political paper, and I'm trying to sell more travelogues to other markets. The more you get your name out there, the more people recognize you and will actually call you to write stories about their cities and venues."

Pitch New Angles

When pitching story ideas, try to come up with new angles on tried-and-true destination stories. Instead of pitching Paris as the city for lovers or "April in Paris," pitch it as a great family destination. Come up with new ideas for fun family vacations or suggest weekend getaways with a different twist. Harper concentrates on tightly focused stories rather than general service-oriented ones. "Each story usually has a very sharp, narrow angle like going to Rome with kids or going narrow boating on the English canal," says Harper. "I don't like to do the whole big encompassing story because they're so hard to sell. Don't try to take some big topic—pick some narrow little slice of what you're doing that has a specific thing to do that might have general interest. Maybe it's a certain type of museum, a certain walk through the volcanoes, or something that has a bit of a twist to it that is pretty specific."

Also, ask markets for editorial calendars. Many travel magazines plan their issues or predetermine what destinations they'll cover months in advance. By reviewing their guidelines, you can pitch ideas that match their needs, or suggest stories that complement their plans.

Explore the Locale

If you've spent any time traveling, you probably already know that there's a certain amount of sameness in many locations. As a travel writer, your job is to find the details that make a location or experience unique and share them with your reader. In other words, find the details that most effectively describe the experience of being there.

Ask yourself, how is this hotel or restaurant or beach or ski resort or cruise ship different from others that are similar to it? You may have to come up with some pretty subtle differences, but keep it in mind as you're traveling and then later, writing the piece. This is where paying attention to all five senses and taking detailed notes will help you later. You also have to be willing to explore, and be open to new experiences.

"The people are a big part of it, as is your willingness to go off the beaten path," says Milivojevic. "You have to get out of the resort and go into that small fishing village and hang around and be open and talk to people. What kind of music are they listening to? What kinds of spices do they use for their food? What do they eat? When do they eat? What's the vibe? Do you feel welcome? Comfortable? Intimidated? All of those come rushing at you if you go off by yourself to a non-tourist place."

Tale from the Front: Kathy Landis

Kathleen Landis of Orangevale, California has been writing about travel as a freelancer for 20 years. She started out writing for regional parenting magazines and regional newspapers and has now written for dozens of publications including *American Way, Country Living, Coastal Living, Diversion* and Subaru's *Drive* magazine. Her tips for travel writers include the following:

Buy a camera and use it. Photographs increase the value of your travel articles, particularly when you're writing for newspapers. Learn the basics of photography early on.

Pitch a travel column to your local newspaper if it doesn't already have one. Landis began writing a column for a regional newspaper which led to dozens of clips and opened a lot of doors for her; scouting for ideas also led to stories for other publications.

Network. Attending press trips, meetings, writer's conferences and other events can lead to great connections and more work. Landis met another writer on a press trip who hooked her up with a guidebook publisher and she ended up landing a freelance gig from her new connection.

Take advantage of travel, convention and PR people who represent destinations, historical societies, resorts and the like. They know the nuts and bolts of their areas and you can call them or visit their websites for information. And, after taking a trip, send a published clip to those sources you used; it's always appreciated and keeps your name in front of them.

Think of multiple markets for your stories. Landis has resold a number of articles to more than one publication. For example, she sold a piece on some local caverns to a local parenting publication. Thereafter she sold it to *Off Road*, a magazine for 4-wheel drive enthusiasts; again as a lifestyle piece featuring a well-known caver to *US Airways*; once more about interesting finds in caves to *Boy's Life*; and finally to the NY Times syndicate. The story, which originally had paid her $25, has now brought in an additional $3,000 to $4,000.

Practical Pitching:
Tips for Getting your First (or Fifteenth) Assignment

When pitching a travel story, your query should include the following elements:

■ An attention-getting lead, which may be anecdotal or time-oriented in nature

■ Enough information about the topic so that the editor knows why the destination and/or topic will interest her readers

■ Details about how you will approach the piece, including the angle, types of sources you plan to interview, and accompanying sidebars

■ An ISG that explains why you're qualified to write the piece

For an example, look at the following query, which sold to *The Globe and Mail,* a major Toronto newspaper. Note that the writer has used a time peg (the upcoming Merchant Ivory movie) and included plenty of detail about the story topic. Her ISG is actually two paragraphs, where she mentions that she's been living in Shanghai for three years and recently updated a guidebook; she also lists some of her clips as well. Note too that she's included the story; many newspaper markets accept completed travel stories in addition to assigning them. One other thing—why Toronto? The writer had researched possible markets throughout the United States and Canada, and knew that it was one of the airline markets with flights to Shanghai—which the travel editor was no doubt aware of as well.

Dear Ms. Smith,

No other city on earth matches the luster of the Pearl of the Orient. Shanghai is the crown jewel of the New China, a metropolis of 16 million that's dazzling the world with its unparalleled speed and energy and redefining "modern" for the 21st century.

But few people realize that the Pearl of the Orient gleamed just as brightly during the late 1930s, when this infamous port city was synonymous with pleasure, power and money. The upcoming Merchant Ivory film The White Countess, opening in January, takes moviegoers back to those decadent days of mansions and mobsters, "singsong clubs" (brothels) and stylish qipaos.

Director James Ivory confessed during filming that it was extremely difficult to recreate old Shanghai amid the futuristic skyscrapers, gridlocked highways and endless high-rises going up at record speed. But the old Shanghai, or at least the spirit of it, still exists – if you know where to look for it.

"Shanghai Surprise" will take The Globe and Mail's readers on a trip down Shanghai's memory lanes: down the plane-tree-lined avenues of the French Concession, past the grand European-style buildings of the Bund. I'll suggest a complete itinerary of walking tours, hotels, restaurants and shops, all of which preserve the spirit of 1930s Shanghai. Air Canada's daily direct flight between Toronto and Shanghai makes the trip an easy, and convenient, one for The Globe and Mail's readers.

As an experienced freelance writer who has lived in Shanghai for three years, I know these surprises of Old Shanghai quite well. I researched them in detail while writing Fodor's Beijing & Shanghai, which was released in January and is now in its second printing.

I've been fortunate to write for a wide variety of publications, including Continental, Sunset, Family Circle, National Geographic Kids and People, among others. (I'd be happy to e-mail clips upon your request.) All of my editors can attest to my ability to turn in clean, creative and concise stories on deadline.

I've pasted "Shanghai Surprise" below for your consideration. If you're interested in the story, I'm happy to send the accompanying photos your way and to further cater the "If You Go" box according to your specifications.

Thanks so much for your time and consideration. If you have any questions, please don't hesitate to email me at kbrwriter_abroad@yahoo.com. I look forward to hearing from you!

Sincerely,
Kristin Baird Rattini

The Markets: Where to Sell Travel

While regional and national newspapers used to be one of the most lucrative markets for travel, most papers are buying fewer travels stories from freelancers. There are still plenty of markets for travel writing available, but new writers may have to start at the bottom with small, local publications and get some clips before pitching to the better-paying markets. Some of the markets for travel stories include:

Travel-specific magazines—these publications specifically cover travel but their audiences vary; *Arthur Frommer's Budget Travel* has a different slant than *Travel & Leisure*, for example.

General interest magazines—most publications include travel stories that may be geared to seasonal topics.

Women's and men's magazines—these magazines often cover travel, usually from a service-oriented angle.

Parenting magazines—cover travel, specifically taking trips with children and family-friendly destinations.

Health and fitness magazines—cover travel including destination pieces, spas and resorts, adventure travel and other related stories.

Cooking/food magazines—these publications often include travel stories, usually with a cooking or food angle.

In-flights—a good market for travel stories; make sure that your destination is one covered by the airline that publishes the magazine.

Travel-oriented web sites—these sites cover travel; as with other online publications, stories tend to run shorter than in print markets and include quizzes, links to other sites and other interactive features.

National/major newspapers—most still do buy freelance travel pieces; some want queries while others want the completed manuscript.

Regional/city magazines and newspapers—like their national counterparts, regional and city publications also publish travel stories, many with a local angle.

Other Useful Stuff

When planning a trip or a travel story, contact the local convention and visitor's bureau for information; if you're traveling to an international destination, get in touch with the country's tourism board or other association or agency for background information, statistics, story ideas, and the like. Most places will also provide photos free of charge. Other potential resources for travel writers are listed below:

Associations/Organizations

American Hotel and Lodging Association
1201 New York Avenue N.W., #600
Washington, D.C. 20005-3931
Phone: 202-289-3100
www.ahma.com
The association serves the hospitality industry and provides a variety of services to members.

American Society of Travel Agents
1101 King St. #200
Alexandria, VA 22314-2944
703-739-2782
www.astanet.com
The 20,000-member organization is the largest association of travel professionals.

Destination Marketing Association International
2025 M St. N.W. #500
Washington, D.C. 20036-3349
202-296-7888
www.destinationmarketing.org/
The association includes more than 1,300 travel- and tourism-related businesses, convention and meeting professionals, and tour operators.

International Association of Amusement Parks and Attractions
1448 Duke Street
Alexandria, VA 22314
703-836-4800
www.iaapa.org
The association includes 4,500 member amusement park/attraction companies.

National Business Travel Association
110 North Royal Street, 4th Floor
Alexandria, VA 22314
Phone: 703-684-0836
www.nbta.org
The NBTA consists of more than 2,500 corporate travel managers and travel service providers.

Travel Industry Association of America
1100 New York Avenue N.W. #450
Washington, D.C.
202-408-8422
www.tia.org
   The association consists of business, professional and trade associations of the travel industry as well as state and local associations that promote tourism to a specific region or site.

Writers Organizations and Other Resources

International Food, Wine and Travel Writers Association
1142 South Diamond Bar Boulevard #177
Diamond Bar, CA 91765
877-439-8929
www.ifwtwa.org
   This 300-member organization consists of professional food, wine and travel journalists in 28 countries.

Professional Outdoor Media Association
P.O. Box 1569
Johnstown, PA 15904
814-254-4719
www.professionaloutdoormedia.org/
   This organization consists of media professionals and corporate partners interested in hunting, fishing, and outdoor recreation.

Outdoor Writers Association of America
1212 Hickory St., No. 1
Missoula, MT 59801
Phone: 406-728-7434
www.owaa.org
   This organization consists of writers and photographers who cover outdoor recreation and conservation topics.

Society of American Travel Writers
1500 Sunday Drive, Suite 102
Raleigh, NC 27607
Phone: 919-861-5586
www.satw.org
   This organization includes 1,300 members who are writers, editors, broadcasters, photographers, and public relations representatives.

Travel Journalists Guild (TJG)
P.O. Box 10643
Chicago, IL 60610
Phone: 312-664-9279
www.tjgonline.com/
   This 75-member organization consists of independent travel writers.

World Federation of Journalists and Travel Writers
c/o Don Bonhaus
One Ballinswood Road
Atlantic Highlands, NJ 07716-1510
Phone: 732-291-2840
www.fijet-web.com/
   This 900-member organization consists of travel journalists throughout the world.

Books

   Lonely Planet Guide to Travel Writing, by Don George (Lonely Planet Publications, 2005). Helpful info about travel-writing; includes interviews with many established travel writers.
   The Travel Writer's Handbook, 5th Edition: How to Write and Sell your Own Travel Experiences, by Louise Purwin Zobel (Surrey Books, 2002). Eighteen chapters cover all aspects of travel writing, including research, pitching, and crafting stories as well as business issues.
   Travel Writing: A Guide to Research, Writing and Selling, by L. Peat O'Neill (Writer's Digest Books, 2005). This nine-chapter comprehensive guide is a good intro to travel writing.

Get off the Couch:
Writing About Fitness and Sports

Can you tell your traps from your tris? Are you the first at your gym to sign up for a new cardio class? Is fitness an important part of your life? If it is, you already know that fitness is no longer merely a component of health. In fact, there are now entire magazines devoted to fitness aimed at women, men, children, older Americans, and even young mothers-to-be. Most general interest magazines also feature fitness-related articles of some form tucked away in every issue.

In addition to straightforward fitness writing, most spectator and participatory sports have at least one magazine—usually many more—for enthusiasts. Local and regional publications are often searching for talented sportswriters to cover events. If you're a sports buff, writing about this field can enable you to develop a specialty about something you love—and give you an insider's look into the sport, the players and the coaches as well.

If you're new to writing about sports, your local paper is one of the best places to start—the editor there may need stringers, or newspaper freelancers, to cover local events. Don't be afraid to pitch profile ideas as well, or to look for sports-themed ideas you can query other markets with. Fitness writers may have an easier time breaking in with short pieces on recent research, how-to tips, or new product write-ups.

One of the best ways to crack this market is to pitch an idea that you have personal experience with. Let's say you're a regular gym buff. Here are a few ideas you might query markets with:

■ A short piece on gym etiquette for a woman's magazine;

■ A story on what to consider when joining a fitness club for a local publication—with a sidebar listing local health clubs

■ A story on indoor interval training techniques for a fitness magazine

■ A story on the popularity of women-only fitness clubs for a business publication

■ A how-to piece on the best 30-minute workout for a men's magazine.

With any luck, you'll get great story ideas as you get—or stay—in great shape!

The Nuts and Bolts: How to Write about Fitness and Sports

Know Your Subject

If you're the world's biggest "super-fan," you've got a leg up when it comes to writing about this field—the key to writing about sports is knowing about them. Just ask freelancer Debbie Elicksen, who covers hockey from Calgary, Alberta, and has turned a lifelong love affair with hockey into a full-time career. She's also the author of books including *Inside the NHL Dream* (Freelance Communications, 2002) and runs a sports blog at http://insideprofessionalsports.blogspot.com. "Since I was a kid, I pretty much was consumed by hockey and lived, breathed, and ate it," says Elicksen. "Even when I was 11, I was confident that I knew more about hockey than most people in the business. If you don't know about it, research the hell out of it and pretend like you do."

When Elicksen accepted a position as PR director for the Edmonton Trappers, a baseball team, she didn't know much about baseball but she learned quickly. "Before I went to Edmonton, I probably took every single book that was available and read it from front to cover," she says. "I became an expert in baseball within the span of two weeks."

Chuck Bednar, a freelancer from Wintersville, Ohio, agrees that a solid background in sports is paramount. "First of all, know something about the sport you intend to cover," says Bednar. "You don't need to be an expert but you do need to understand what you're seeing." If you don't understand the rules of the game or the nuances of the sport, it will be impossible to communicate with your readers, regardless of the sport you're covering.

Start Off Small

You say you want to write for *Sports Illustrated*? That's great, but you'll probably have to start at the bottom and build your clips before you nail an assignment from one of the major sports publications. "Don't even think about trying for the major markets like *ESPN* and *Sports Illustrated* until you're well-established," says Bednar. "It's a sad but true fact that these markets are a lot tougher to crack than most people believe. Likewise, drop the pretense that you can talk to a Barry Bonds or a Michael Jordan right off the bat."

Instead, set your sights on smaller publications when you're starting out. Bednar suggests that freelancers break in by contacting their local paper to see if the sports editor needs any correspondents or "stringers" to cover sports events. Learning how to keep score is a valuable asset as well. When you approach national magazines, consider pitching unique stories that they don't have access to. "Look around your community for local success stories and stories of people overcoming the odds—things a national audience would be interested in but wouldn't be exposed to if you didn't write it," says Bednar, who started covering sports in high school and college for student newspapers. By the time he was in college, he was writing for the local paper and racking up clips.

Develop a Network of Sources

Sports writing can be a very difficult industry to get into. It takes a while for writers to gain credibility. "The tendency seems to be to gravitate toward the people who have been there for a while. That's how I helped myself when I got started—I pretty much got to know everybody in the industry while I was in it," says Elicksen. She made a point of befriending scouts, security guards, dressing room attendants, and team employees when she first started writing about hockey, and her efforts have paid off.

"I tried to get in tight, and some are now very good friends of mine," she says. "The more people you get to know, the more you know what's going on. And again, the more you know about the industry, and the more you learn about the industry, the easier it is to write."

When interviewing athletes, it's important that you know more that just an athlete's latest accomplishment or commercial appearance. Familiarize yourself with his or her statistics and career history and memorize a few of the lesser-known facts to mention in the interview, suggests Cindy BeMent, a freelancer in Warsaw, Indiana who writes about fitness. "For example, you could ask something like, 'even though this is your first professional marathon, you ran the New York City Marathon on a dare when you were 18. Tell me more about that'," says

BeMent. "These facts are harder to find, but if you dig you can come up with them and they can make for a more colorful interview session. Also, get to know some of the lingo of the sport, but don't stretch beyond your comfort level in using it in an interview, lest you make yourself look less knowledgeable."

Keep Your Finger on the Pulse

When you're writing about sports and fitness, you also have to keep up on what's happening. Keep in touch with your network of sources. Track the latest trends—in the fitness world, yoga, Pilates and group classes like Spinning were immensely popular in the early 2000s. Today there's a big emphasis on mind-body fitness, "functional" fitness, and balanced workout programs.

When covering your favorite sports teams, ask to be included on their media and fan lists; you can track what's happening and come up with new story ideas that way. If writing about general fitness, trade associations like IDEA Health and Fitness Association, the American Council on Exercise and the Aerobic and Fitness Association of America can help keep you abreast of new trends and training ideas.

Use Your Background

You needn't be an aerobics instructor to write fitness-related articles, but being a marathoner or weekend warrior certainly doesn't hurt. Cindy BeMent used her fitness background—she's a certified personal trainer and competitive runner—to enter the freelancing world. While she'd done some sports writing in college, throughout her career she had focused in sales and marketing. When she started freelancing, however, she found that her running background and fitness experience gave her "a leg up" over other writers.

"Writing about running and fitness was a natural entrée into freelancing for me," says BeMent. "I get a steady stream of ideas coming my way from questions, problems and successes my running students encounter. Plus, I run for sport, so I know the lingo and the proper channels to go through to get access to the pros. That combination made me attractive to editors, even though I didn't have a stack of clips in the beginning."

Follow Your Heart (and Your Heart Rate)

Another key to writing about sports and fitness is to find an area that you enjoy. "Definitely find an area of sports and fitness that you are interested in yourself," says BeMent. "There's always the 'write what you know,' but I don't mean that. I mean write what you are very curious about."

"'Write what you know' is a standard," agrees Tom Bedell, who writes about golf, travel and beer from Williamsville, Vermont. "Instead, write what you know about or would like to know about." Bedell started writing about golf in the mid-90s, when he says he realized that the only way to play as much as he wanted was to start writing about it as well. He's successfully created a niche for himself and enjoys covering a variety of golf-related subjects like golf course architecture for regional and national publications.

Consider the Playing Fields

Whether you're writing about sports or fitness, you'll want to keep the market in mind when pitching story ideas. Consider women's magazines. While nearly every one runs fitness-related articles, mainstream publications like *Family Circle* and *Woman's Day* tend to feature walking workouts or simpler exercises while magazines like *Self, Shape* and *Fitness* offer more cutting-edge and complex regimes.

Because of that, it's smart to study the fitness and sports markets you want to write for before you query. How are the articles structured? How broad is the coverage area? What kinds of experts are featured? By getting a good feel for what the markets are looking for, you'll increase your chances of getting an assignment.

"When writing about fitness, think helpful, fresh and different," says BeMent. "Really work to find new research and experts with credible backgrounds to help inform your articles. That said, don't be afraid of revisiting a basic topic. As with any good habits we hope to form in life, fitness writing can sometimes serve to refresh and remind its audience about sound principles and safe practices. See if there is a new angle to an old topic or further studies that could update a particular standard subject."

Stretch Yourself

Many savvy sports and fitness writers eventually expand their niches and begin covering other areas as well. Writing about sports and travel is a natural combination, as is using your fitness background to branch into health or nutrition. "You can write about sports for a while, and if you're a savvy enough marketer, you can segue into some other things," says BeMent. "I started more on the running end and sport and then I had to get some more general health clips. One way to steer myself that way was to write about running features and then write about related items like injury prevention and nutrition for that running publication. That way you can kind of bounce over into other stuff."

Get Your Name out

As mentioned before, when you're starting out and you're short on fitness or sports clips, consider pitching to local or regional publications. Bedell wrote his first golf article for a statewide magazine, *Vermont Golf,* and then nailed additional assignments for other regional publications like *New York Golf* and *New Hampshire Golf,* which are produced by the same publisher. He then leapfrogged to in-flights and travel magazines.

You can also create visibility for yourself and develop clips by writing a sports or fitness column for a local or regional publication, says Bedell, who is the golf columnist for his local daily newspaper. "It doesn't pay much but it's local and I probably get more feedback from that than anything else I do," says Bedell. "And there's a bit of synergy in everything we do. What I write for local paper sometimes becomes research for a larger story, and it helped me learn more about what was becoming my specialty, which was golf."

If you don't have a website, you may want to consider having a blog instead—it can be an easier way to build your platform and get your name out to potential editors and clients. Debbie Elicksen's blog, "Inside the Locker Room: Behind the Scenes' Look at Professional Sports" (http://insideprofessionalsports.blogspot.com/) includes entries that first appeared in print in magazines. Freelancer Claire Walter, profiled below, maintains three separate blogs in three different subject areas. A blog is often cheaper and easier to update than a website, and more writers are using them to both showcase and build an audience for their work.

Tales from the Front: Claire Walter

Claire Walter of Boulder, Colorado was a magazine editor at *Ski* and worked in public relations handling ski accounts before she began freelancing in 1970s. Covering skiing—and eventually other snow sports—was a natural specialty for her. Since then, she's branched out and also writes about food, fitness and travel as well; she's the author of hundreds of magazine articles and numerous books including *Snowshoeing Colorado* (Fulcrum Publishing), *The Snowshoe Experience* (Storey Publishing) and *Culinary Colorado* (Fulcrum Publishing). Her next book, *Nordic Walking: Pole Your Way to Fitness,* will be published in 2008 by Hatherleigh Press.

She offers this advice for writers who want to write about fitness or sports:

Walk the walk. You need to participate in the activity unless you're writing about something like pro hockey or pro football. When you're writing about something that is a participatory activity, you may miss some obvious aspects of the sport if you don't participate. "I think that's one of the real no-nos," says Walter. "You kind of miss the flavor of what people really do and are concerned about, and what it is like. For example, I wouldn't dream about writing about golf because I don't golf."

Keep up to date. It's important to stay up on what's happening in the area you cover. Subscribing to trade magazines or other publications or websites geared to people in the business of what you cover can help you pick up on trends and determine whether you're writing about activities that are gaining popularity and gathering interest—or not. Attend trade shows, if you can, and keep up with what people in the industry are reading. "If you are plugged into the industry, whatever it is, and you pick up on these trends, you might be the first person to write about the trend," says Walter, who wrote *Snowshoeing Colorado* (Fulcrum, 1998) after realizing how popular the sport had become. "If I had not been paying attention to that fact, someone else would have written that book." *Snowshoeing Colorado* is in its third edition, and Walter believes that Nordic walking will be a popular fitness activity for the 21st century.

Network. Join writers' organizations like the American Society of Journalists and Authors (ASJA) and any specialized organizations in your field. "If you're writing about hunting and fishing, join the Outdoor Writers," says Walter. "If you're writing about travel, join the Travel Journalists Guild or the Society of Travel Writers. If you're writing about skiing and snow sports like I am, join the North American Snow Sports Journalism Association." Membership in these organizations keeps you in the loop and can lead to assignments as well.

Invest in yourself. "When people start freelancing, they're often pennywise and pound foolish," says Walter. "People will buy the cheapest stationery and buy crummy business cards, things that don't look as is they're professional so that they can command a decent fee." Spend the money for quality supplies, and present yourself as a professional—and you'll be treated like one.

Use today's technical tools. No freelance writer with a specialty can be without a website and increasingly a blog. Editors and potential book buyers search the Internet for authorities and information. Walter's website includes her resume, previews of all of her books, and a click-through index to dozens of published articles that are often available for reprints. She also maintains three blogs: http://culinary-colorado.blogspot.com on food topics in Colorado and elsewhere, http://travel-babel.blogspot.com on her own travels and her observations on travel trends, and http://nordic-walking-usa.blogspot.com on Nordic walking, which she's currently writing a book about.

Practical Pitching:
Tips for Getting your First (or Fifteenth) Assignment

When pitching a fitness or sports story, your query should include the following elements:
■ An attention-getting lead, which may be anecdotal or research-oriented (such as quoting a recent study) in nature
■ Enough information about the topic so that the editor knows why the topic will interest her readers
■ Details about how you will approach the piece, including the angle, types of sources you plan to interview, and accompanying sidebars
■ An ISG that explains why you're qualified to write the piece

Take a look at the following fitness query, which sold to www.msnbc.com. Note that the writer has taken an evergreen idea (how to get more from your workouts) and given it a technology spin. He's clearly researched the fitness technology he's pitching, he has personal experience with the subject matter, and he's even peppered the query with sports lingo. You can easily see why it sold.

Hi Jackie:

Nice talking to you on Friday. Here's the story idea:

Taking Workouts to a Higher Level: It's no secret that athletes and exercise buffs face steep challenges when it comes to monitoring performance and staying motivated. Meeting goals for pumping iron, running or biking is no lightweight task. But thanks to a new wave of hi-tech devices that offer monitoring and performance feedback, ordinary people are reaching new heights with their workouts.

Consider: Fitlinxx (www.fitlinxx.com), a computerized training circuit, is making inroads at health clubs and rehab facilities. It lets you establish a customized exercise program that includes cardio and weights. These "connected" devices track performance electronically and feed data into a personal computer. When you use the weight machines, for example, Fitlinxx tracks range of motion, speed and other factors and provides immediate feedback through audible beeps and data on a touch-screen LCD attached to each machine. If you go too fast it tells you to slow down. If you're unable to complete a set, the system prompts you to lower the weights the next time around. On the other hand, if you blast through your goal, it asks you if you'd like to increase the load next time around. You can also view your performance from the previous workout and past sessions to spot overall trends.

The story is the same when you step on a treadmill or exercise bike, Fitlinxx grabs your workout data and sends it to your personal workout log. What's more, you're able to add data about dozens of other activities on your own, including running, walking, gardening, karate, swimming and dancing. At any time, you can view your detailed performance data and accumulated points on a kiosk or PC. Over time, you can win prizes, such as towels, gym bags, medals and more. Fitlinxx claims a 35% higher retention rate than conventional systems.

Yet Fitlinxx isn't the only monitoring system that's changing the face of exercise. The Timex BodyLink system uses a small GPS receiver and heart rate monitor to track speed, distance and exertion levels. It's ideal for runners, bikers and others who want to monitor their exact performance or have specific training goals. Nike's TRIAX Elite (www.nike.com/

nikerunning/index.jhtml) and the FitSense (www.fitsense.com) body monitoring system also offer precise data about pacing, speed, calories burned and heart rate. These devices, which use sophisticated accelerometers to measure motion and incorporate wireless systems to feed data from a chip attached to a shoe to a watch, also include software for maintaining a log or sending data to a Web site (via a small device that connects to a PC) so that it's possible to view charts, splits and much more. The final score? While these hi-tech gadgets do not make workouts any easier, they're helping a growing number of people reach the finish line.

As I mentioned, I've been using Fitlinxx at the local YMCA for the last couple of months and I'm very impressed. I've been lifting weights for years and the Fitlinxx system forces a person to exercise correctly (lift the weights slowly, use the proper range of motion, use correct seat settings and adjustments, etc.). I've also used FitSense for the last year in my marathon training. It's proven invaluable in terms of establishing target speeds for different types of runs and getting real-time feedback about whether I'm hitting my target pace that day. It's also great for spotting overall patterns over days, weeks and months.

Best,
Samuel Greengard

The Markets: Where to Sell Fitness

There's no shortage of markets for fitness and sports-related stories, but pay rates vary widely. While national magazines will pay $1/word and up for fitness features and sports articles, smaller and more specialized magazines and markets may pay much less. Near the bottom of the pile are the newspapers; your local paper may pay only $25 to $50 for a sports feature, but these clips can be invaluable when you're entering this field.

Some of the biggest markets for fitness and sports-related writing and their areas of interest include:

Fitness magazines—there are a wide variety of magazines, both national and regional, dedicated to covering fitness topics as well as health, nutrition and lifestyle subjects.

Sports magazines—nearly every sport has several magazines aimed specifically at fans, participants, and devotees. While these publications have a narrower range of interest, they can offer an opportunity for newer freelancers to break in.

General interest magazines—these often cover fitness and sport topics whether it is the latest fitness trend or a profile of a famous athlete or sports team.

Professional and trade journals—trade journals for fitness professionals, health club owners, athletic trainers, and other related medical specialties all offer opportunities for writers in this area.

Women's and men's magazines—these magazines cover a broad range of fitness- and sports- related subjects, mostly service-oriented. Both types of magazines include general fitness pieces as well as workout stories; men's magazines may also include sports profiles and other sport-related subjects.

Parenting magazines—cover children's fitness and well-being and youth sports as part of covering children's health in general.

Cooking/food magazines—many magazines also cover fitness-related subjects, often focusing on service.

Fitness-related and sports web sites—while some markets cover a variety of fitness topics, others may limit themselves to addressing a specific sport. As with other online publications, stories tend to run shorter than in print markets and include quizzes, links to other sites and fun interactive features.

National/major newspapers—cover fitness topics as well as sports.

Regional/city magazines and newspapers—like their national counterparts, regional and city publications also cover a broad range of fitness-related topics, many with a regional angle, as well as local sports.

Other Useful Stuff

So, how do you find experts for a fitness story or locate an association of writers who cover a particular sport? Some useful organizations and resources are listed below:

Online Resources:

InteliHealth, www.intelihealth.com. Offers free email newsletters on a variety of fitness-related topics; also includes basic fitness information.

Newswise, www.newswise.com. Newswise offers free email newletters on fitness-related subjects, maintains press releases and an online directory of experts.

Profnet, profnet.prnewswire.com. Search the online database or submit a query to find experts in particular areas; you must be a published freelancer and register to use the service.

PubMed, www.ncbi.nlm.nih.gov/PubMed. PubMed provides online access to the National Library of Medicine, which includes fitness-related research articles.

Reuters Health, www.reutershealth.com. Site that includes daily news releases about fitness, health, and nutrition.

Associations/Organizations

Aerobics and Fitness Association of America

15250 Ventura Blvd., Suite 200
Sherman Oaks, CA 91403
Phone: 818-905-0040 or 800-446-AFAA
www.afaa.com

This 155,000-member association promotes safety and excellence in exercise instruction; provides certification in aerobics, personal training, and other fitness specialties.

American College of Sports Medicine

401 W. Michigan St.
Indianapolis, IN 46202-3233
Phone: 317-637-9200
www.acsm.org

This 20,000-member organization includes members in a wide range of medical specialties who seek to maintain and improve physical performance, fitness, health and quality of life.

American Running Association
4405 East-West Highway, Suite 405
Bethesda, MD 20814
Phone: 301-913-9517 or 800-776-ARFA
www.americanrunning.org

This 15,000-member organization consists of runners, exercise enthusiasts, and sports medicine professionals.

Cooper Institute for Aerobic Research
12330 Preston Road
Dallas, TX 75230
Phone: 972-341-3200 or 800-635-7050
www.cooperinst.org/

The institute conducts research on living habits and health; offers advice on how to change living habits and develop positive life skills.

Exercise Safety Association
P.O. Box 547916
Orlando, FL 32854-7916
Phone: 407- 246-5090
www.exercisesafety.com

The ESA includes fitness instructors, personal trainers, health spas, YMCAs, community recreation departments and hospital wellness programs.

IDEA Health and Fitness Association
10455 Pacific Center Court
San Diego, CA 92121-4339
Phone: 800-999-IDEA
www.ideafit.com

This 18,000-member organization provides continuing education for fitness professionals, personal trainers, program directors and club/studio owners.

National Association for Health and Fitness
c/o Be Active New York State
65 Niagara Square, Room 607
Buffalo, NY 14202
Phone: 716.583.0521
www.physicalfitness.org/

This non-profit organization seeks to improve quality of life by promoting physical fitness, sports and healthy lifestyles; works with governor's and state councils that promote and encourage regular physical activity.

National Athletic Trainers Association

2952 Stemmons Freeway, Suite 200
Dallas, TX 75247-6196
Phone: 214-637-6282 or 800-879-6282
www.nata.org

This 30,000-member organization consists of athletic trainers from universities and colleges, professional sports, military establishments, sports medicine clinics, and business/industrial health programs.

National Collegiate Athletic Association

700 W. Washington St.
P.O. Box 6222
Indianapolis, IN 46206-6222
Phone: 317-917-6222
www.ncaa.org

The NCAA consists of university, college and allied educational athletics associations devoted to the administration of intercollegiate athletics.

National Strength and Conditioning Association

1885 Bob Johnson Drive
Colorado Springs, CO 80906
Phone: 719-632-6722 or 800-815-6826
www.nsca-lift.org

This 29,000-member organization is made up of professionals in sports science, athletic and fitness industries, and promotes conditioning to prevent injury.

Writers Organizations and Other Resources

Association for Women in Sports Media

ESPN
ESPN Plaza
Bristol, CT 06010
Phone: 860-766-7639
www.awsmonline.org/

This 600-member organization is made up of female sportswriters, copy editors, broadcasters and media relations directors.

Baseball Writers Association of America

P.O. Box 610611
Bayside, NY 11361
Phone: 718-767-2582
www.baseballwriters.org/

Membership in this organization is restricted to sports writers on direct assignment to major league baseball.

Football Writers Association of America

18652 Vista Del Sol
Dallas, TX 75287
Phone: 972-713-6198
hwww.fwaa.com

This 850-member organization consists of newspaper and magazine writers who cover high school, college and professional football.

Golf Writers Association of America

10210 Greentree Road
Houston, TX 77042-1232
Phone: 713-782-6664
gwaa.com

This 900-member association includes editors and writers who cover golf.

National Sportscasters and Sportswriters Association

322 E. Innes Ct.
Salisbury, NC 28144
Phone: 704-633-4275

This 1,000-member organization consists of sportscasters and sportswriters; operates the National Sportscaster and Sportswriters Hall of Fame.

North American Snow Sports Journalists Association

P.O. Box 74563
2803 West 4th Avenue
Vancouver, British Columbia, Canada V6K4P4
Phone: 604-877-1141
www.nasja.org

The association consists of 300 writers of ski-related news, information and features throughout the U.S. and Canada.

Professional Hockey Writers Association
1480 Pleasant Valley Way, No. 44
West Orange, CA 07052
Phone: 973-669-8607
The 400-member association consists of writers who cover member teams of the National Hockey League.

United States Basketball Writers Association
1000 St. Louis Union Station, Suite 105
St. Louis, MO 63103
Phone: 314-421-0339
www.sportswriters.net/usbwa/index.html
This 1,000-member organization includes writers who cover college and professional basketball.

Books

Associated Press Sports Writing Handbook, by Steve Wilstein (McGraw Hill, 2002). Nuts and bolts advice on sports-writing, lots of "war stories" and advice from noted sports writers, examples of outstanding beat reporting, columns, etc.

The Sports Writing Handbook, Second Edition, by Thomas Fensch (Lawrence Erlbaum Associates, 1995). Good guide to sports writing; includes chapters on interviewing, leads, advance articles, sports features and extensive list of sports teams.

Warm Your Heart:
Writing Essays and Personal Pieces

The overwhelming success of the *Chicken Soup for the Soul* series of books reveals an almost limitless audience for short inspirational and heartwarming pieces, but essays can be humorous, political, or satirical as well. A talented essay writer can command high rates—$2/word and up—from national publications. And because of the nature of the form, essays offer a chance for nonfiction freelancers to write something a little different than usual—and profit from it, too.

Yet essays often appear to be easier to write than they really are. They're also unusual in that you don't query an editor with an essay; rather, you write the piece and send it in with a cover letter. Read on for the keys to successfully writing compelling essays—and getting paid for them as well.

The Nuts and Bolts: How to Write Essays

Think Beyond Yourself

First and most important, understand that a good essay does more than relate a personal event or share your thoughts, opinions or feelings with your readers. It can't consist of merely your own experience—it must be broad enough for complete strangers to get something out of it. "You've got to personalize and at the same time universalize what you're saying so that other people can relate to what you're saying and agree or disagree with it," says essay writer Susan J. Gordon of White Plains, New York, who has sold essays to publications including *Woman's Day, Parents, Working Mother* and *Good Housekeeping.*

"Just telling about an experience in your life or an insight you had isn't enough for the majority of editors and readers," agrees Kathryn Lay, a freelancer in Arlington, Texas who's sold more than 700 essays and personal experience stories. "You need to find a way others can relate. Compare your experience to an emotion, a desire, a frustration, a need, or something [else]."

Let Yourself be Unique

Unlike writing an assigned article, crafting essays offers an opportunity to stretch creatively and take risks you might not in a reported or how-to story. After all, when you write for magazines, you try to match the voice and the sensibility of the publication. With an essay, your voice is your own. "The value of the personal essay is how much it reflects your own personal, really unique voice. I describe a personal essay as something in which your own voice is one of the dominant features of it," says Cleveland-based freelancer Kristin Ohlson, author of *Stalking the Divine* (Plume, 2004.) "That's one of the things that people are drawn to—or not drawn to—about the piece."

In addition, writing an essay gives you freedom as far as structure goes. You don't have to write a 1,500-word piece with two sidebars because that's what was assigned. You can write as long—or as short—as you like, and then worry about finding a market for your piece when you're finished. "Essays are in your own voice, and they are your own making," says Ohlson. "You make the structure, you make the length, you make everything about it, and that's a little different [from articles]...for that reason sometimes they are a wonderful way for other people to see how you can write."

Consider Your Audience

Writing the essay and then finding a home for it lets you keep your options open. On the other hand, some successful essay writers think of their audience and consider the message they want to communicate before they begin writing. "Think about what the market is and who your audience is," says Gordon. "You always have to speak to that particular reader and pay attention to that. What works for me is finding ways to make my personal story meaningful to others. You shouldn't talk about yourself unless you've got a way to let the reader in."

In fact, too many unpublished essayists think only about what they want to write, not what people want to read about. Even if you write the piece primarily for yourself, you have to consider your eventual readers as well—at least if you want to publish your work. Sharon Cindrich, a freelancer in Wauwatosa, Wisconsin, always keeps her audience in mind when writing essays. "Your audience has to identify with you and your story—to see themselves or at least part of themselves in the picture," says Cindrich, who writes essays and nonfiction articles. "Even though the piece may seem to be about me and my experience, my goal is that my audience will immediately see it as a story about themselves. They might see themselves in a new light, with a humorous perspective or gain a new understanding from it."

Start with a Sideline

While essay-writing can be a profitable sideline, few writers can support themselves writing essays alone. As a result, many freelancers write essays for the enjoyment and occasional checks, but rely on nonfiction articles and books to pay the bills. "It's very difficult to make a living just doing essay writing for commercial magazines," says Andrea Cooper, a freelancer in Charlotte, North Carolina. "For one thing, the opportunities at each magazine tend to be much more limited. They'll have the back page essay and a million articles."

Essays also often take much longer to write than non-fiction articles, and the process may not be as straightforward. "With service pieces [such as how-to articles], you know what they want—10 ways to do this or that, and you do it in a very organized way. You sit down and you get your interviews and put the piece together and it's done," says Gordon. "Essays take a lot of time, and they can percolate for months. You can't churn them out."

Expand Your Market Awareness

You'll increase your chances of selling and publishing your essays if you look for markets that are a good match for your writing style. While most publications have at least one essay slot, many magazines tend to run the same kinds of pieces over and over. Not surprisingly, a parenting magazine will publish essays on the joys and challenges of raising kids while a magazine aimed at seniors will run stories that reflect issues its readers face. Consider what the market publishes before you send in your work.

"A fair number of magazines can be pretty conservative in what they take," says Cooper. "One of the lessons I've learned as an essayist is that you really need to look for places that are running pieces that you really admire and that you wish you had written. There are just some places that are going to be a better philosophical match for you. Go to the newsstand and see who is publishing what in terms of the complexity of the subject matter, the tone, and are they essays that require a depth of research or purely from your own experience. You have to match yourself reasonably well to the publication."

Because the markets for essays may be more limited, it makes sense to look for publications close to home as you begin your essay-writing career. Cindrich, who used to live in a Chicago suburb, first published her essays in *The Chicago Tribune* and a regional publication called *West Suburban Living*. While she now lives outside Milwaukee, she continues to write a regular column for *West Suburban Living* but writes for both national and regional publications as well. "Think global, but act local," says Cindrich. "On a national level, you're competing with thousands for a handful of slots. Look into local newspapers, regional mags, newsletters, et cetera for markets."

Do Your Homework

The great thing about writing essays is that you can simply sit down and write off the top of your head—no research is necessary, right? Wrong. Even for a personal essay, it's often helpful to conduct some research about a topic before you start writing about it. You may use the information you find out as background or incorporate and weave it into the piece itself. The result can be a more thoughtful and compelling essay.

"I've always found that doing research even for a personal essay is very important," says Cooper. "With a personal essay when you're writing about your own experience, you always run the risk of people looking at this and saying, 'who cares?' I've found that the research helps me broaden it out somewhat."

Choose Your Material Carefully

If you're writing a nonfiction article, it doesn't really matter how you feel about the subject matter. The fact that ways to cut your household bills or tax-saving tips doesn't excite you is irrelevant. The opposite is true when writing essays—if you don't have strong feelings about something, your essay will probably be weak. "It's not enough to know about something," says Gordon. "You must also care—and care deeply—about the topic."

You can't just vent your spleen and call it an essay, either. "I teach creative writing sometimes too, so I'm telling my students [that essays ae] not just their opportunity to hold forth on the war in Iraq," says Ohlson. Instead, essay-writing requires "really reflecting on something deeply personal that's happened and trying somehow to get at the mystery of why there's something moving about it," she says. "For me, the things that have turned out to be successful personal essays where when there was something that happened in my life with the people around me that all of a sudden struck me—in some way I was moved by it, and I thought, this is something that bears greater reflection."

Your essay should also offer readers something new. "With essays, the writing is everything," agrees Cooper. "You have to have original ideas and be able to express them in a way that makes people notice. It's creating an experience for someone who doesn't know you but who will want to be with you because of the experience you're creating together."

Keep an Idea Journal

Sometimes with essays an idea may spring full-blown, but it's a good idea to keep a running list of potential story ideas. "One thing I encourage is to keep a personal experience journal," says Lay, who teaches essay writing. "This would include an experience that happens, along with details, senses, and how it affected them and might encourage, challenge, inform, entertain, or surprise readers."

Cindrich often jots notes for essay ideas on her calendar alongside her children's doctor's appointments, after-school activities, and birthday parties. "It doesn't always have to be formal or lengthy," she says. "If I have an idea, I jot down a line or phrase or my thought on my kitchen calendar. I may not come back to it for a while but if I need some ideas, I always know I can browse the notes there."

Another effective way of developing new essay ideas is tying in your subject with a seasonal or regular event. "Be fresh. Take an old idea and turn it around," says Gordon. "Think ahead of upcoming holidays and be seasonal." Remember that to place essays for holidays like Mother's Day, Easter, Thanksgiving, and Christmas, you'll want to submit your work well in advance. Timing depends on the market, but send event-oriented essays at least six months ahead of time—competition for those slots is high!

Don't Overdo the Details

One of the most difficult parts of writing essays is staying within word count. When you're writing about something that's really important to you, you may not want to leave anything out, but go overboard with details and you'll lose your reader. Choose wisely and focus on the most important details—the telling details that make the essay.

It also helps if you know how long the essay will be before you begin writing it—at least if you're going to write an essay with a particular market in mind. "It helps to structure your story," says Cindrich. "Research the essay slots or check guidelines if you know you're aiming for a particular publication."

Maximize Reprint Sales

While essays do tend to take more time to write than articles, they offer reprint opportunities as well. Pieces that are closely related to recent events may not sell more than once, but essays on evergreen topics can be resold again and again. For example, Gordon wrote an essay for *McCall's* about her stepfather 15 years ago, and was paid $1,000 for first rights to it. In the years since then, it has been reprinted in the Canadian version of *Readers Digest*, in a textbook, and in *Chicken Soup for the Father's Soul*. All told, she's made more money selling reprints of her essay than she earned in the first place—and will possibly reprint it again.

Of course, you can only offer reprint rights on essays that you own the rights to, so be sure to read your contracts carefully before signing them. If you sign all-rights contracts or "work-for-hires," you're precluded from reselling your work to other markets such as anthologies. However, a prestigious clip from a national magazine might be an investment in your portfolio and a chance at exposure, says Cindrich. "So 'selling out' isn't always a bad thing," she adds. "But consider it carefully and weigh the pros and cons before you sell your soul."

Tales from the Front: Deborah Shouse

Deborah Shouse, a freelancer from Prairie Village, Kansas, has been writing essays for the past 18 years; they've appeared in markets including *Reader's Digest, Woman's Day, Family Circle, Hemispheres,* and *The Christian Science Monitor*. She offers this advice for essay writers:

Write from your heart. Keep your writing visual—that is, write in scenes, so the reader is anchored and can see and sense what is happening.

Keep your essays tightly focused. The greater the focus, the more chance for emotional impact. Add in humor whenever possible. Your goal is to have the reader feel changed by your work.

Be persistent. When you write a piece that you love and feel is good, don't give up. Keep marketing. Shouse has found markets for five-year-old stories after they've been rejected dozens of times. Once they're published, they're often reprinted.

Enjoy the process. "I find this kind of writing wonderful, enriching and humbling," says Shouse. "Humbling because you have no control whether magazines want to publish your most wonderful work. Enriching because you have a chance to understand more deeply about yourself and your life. Wonderful because you are doing a kind of writing that can really move and inspire people."

Practical Pitching:
Tips for Getting your First (or Fifteenth) Assignment

With an essay, you don't send a traditional query; instead, you send the piece itself, along with a brief cover letter. Ideally, the letter should catch the editor's attention and explain why the essay is appropriate for her audience. Look at the example below, which includes a lead to catch the editor's attention, information about the essay itself, and an explanation of why readers of the magazine will appreciate the piece. With an essay, your ISG is of less importance—the essay speaks for itself. The editor will either buy it or not, based not on your experience but on the nature of the piece, whether it moves her, and whether it's right for her readers.

Dear Ms. Jolie:

Did you know that November is National Adoption Month? According to the U.S. Census, there are 1.6 million adopted children under the age of the 18, and 4% of all households contain adopted children. That makes it likely that someone close to you—a friend, a family member, a neighbor, or a coworker—has been touched by adoption.

Yet becoming a parent by adoption differs from doing it the biological way. My enclosed essay, "I'm Having a Baby—Really!," explores this alternate routes to parenthood, describing the excitement—and healing process—of becoming a mom through adoption. I believe your readers will relate to the anticipation of first-time parenthood however they became moms and dads. (My piece has a happy ending, too—my son, Ryan, just turned one.)

Let me know if you have any questions about this essay, and have a great day! Thanks for your time and consideration.

All good things,
Kelly James-Enger

The Markets: Where to Sell Essays and Personal Pieces

There is an enormous variety of markets that publish essays and personal pieces, and they vary widely in audience, scope and focus. Check back issues to see what types of essays are published, how long they are, and what types of topics they are covered, and request a copy of their writers' guidelines before submitting material.

Some of the most popular markets for essays include:

Women's magazines – Women's magazines like *Family Circle*, *Woman's Day* and *Redbook* have all published essays, personal pieces, and humor for years.

Men's magazines – While they don't publish as many essays as the women's publications, men's magazines also publish essays.

Parenting publications – Both national and regional publications run essays, usually to do with some aspect of parenting or child care, often with a humorous twist.

General interest magazines – Most run essays, such as Newsweek's long-running column "My Turn."

Regional and local publications – These smaller markets are often good places for essay writers to gain experience and offer reprint opportunities as well.

In-flight and travel magazines – Both in-flight and travel publications publish essays which range in length and scope.

Religious publications – Religious magazines run many essays and personal experience pieces.

Newspapers – Local, regional and national newspapers all run op/ed pieces and essays in different sections of the papers.

Anthologies – Books such as the *Chicken Soup for the Soul* series all purchase rights to essays and publish collections of them.

Websites – Websites such as www.salon.com also publish essays and personal pieces.

Other Useful Stuff

Essay writing is a unique skill, but one that can be developed. If you want to write essays, it may be helpful to take a class at your local college or sign up for an online course. Joining a writers' group to share and critique your work can help you stay focused and improve your writing skills. There are also a number of books on the craft of essay writing including:

Writing Personal Essays: How to Shape your Life Experiences for the Page, by Sheila Bender (Writer's Digest Books, 1995). Eleven chapters on how to write different types of essays and publish them; includes appendix.

The Essayist at Work: Profiles of Creative Nonfiction Writers, by Lee Gutkind, editor (Heinemann, 1998). Nineteen profiles with noted nonfiction and essay writers; gives insight into the craft of essay-writing.

No Place Like it: Writing About Home and Garden

Do you like to "putter"? Are you known for your homegrown tomatoes? Did you build your backyard deck yourself? As a writer, you're in luck. Entire publications—often called "shelter" magazines—are dedicated to the home and garden niche, and most general interest publications cover these topics as well. Articles may explain how to landscape your backyard, remodel a bathroom, or maximize your storage space.

An interest in these subjects is often a jumping-off point to writing about these specialized areas, and nothing is better than hands-on experience when it comes to pitching story ideas. Thanks to the practical appeal and increasing interest in home improvement and maintenance, these topics are a lucrative area to specialize in, particularly for writers who have a background in home repair or gardening.

If you want to turn your do-it-yourself projects into money-making articles as well, start with subjects you already have hands-on experience with. If you recently remodeled your bathroom, started a container herb garden, or refinanced your condo, look for markets that would be a good match for those ideas. You're a new homeowner? You've probably got more ideas than you know what to do with:

■ A story on buying your first home for a young women's magazine

■ A piece on up-and-coming neighborhoods for a local publication

■ A story on redecorating a kid's room on a budget for a parenting magazine

■ A piece on the pros and cons of reverse mortgages for a senior's magazine

■ A story on home office dos and don'ts for a trade or business publication

The Nuts and Bolts: Writing About Home and Garden

Use Your Background

As with most specialties, you'll find it easier to break into this area if you already have knowledge or experience with the subject. Take Judy Bistany, a freelancer from Columbia, South Carolina. She's an interior designer who covers home design as an associate editor for a regional magazine and freelances as well. Lisa Iannucci, a freelancer in Poughkeepsie, New York, had worked as an editorial assistant at *Home Mechanix*. When she started freelancing, she pitched a story on pregnancy and remodeling, which led to writing a home decorating column for her local paper. She then used that experience to start writing weekly stories about real estate and home remodeling subjects for a larger newspaper.

"I basically learned all of it on the job. If I had to do something on mortgages, I learned about it while writing," says Iannucci. "Little by little, I learned more and more. For example, I'm not an interior decorator but I knew where to find the experts." By using her initial knowledge base as a starting point and interviewing experts, Iannucci was able to branch into related subjects as well. Today she still covers real estate topics in addition to covering television and celebrity-related subjects.

Know Your Subject

You needn't be an expert on home repair or raising prize-winning roses, but you do have to know enough about home and gardening subjects to write about them accurately. "If you're breaking into the interior design market, you have to understand what design is all about," says Bistany. "You have to understand the depth of it and understand what makes it work."

If you're overwhelmed by the subject, start with a relatively simple idea that you have personal experience with. For example, I sold a story on buying your first home to a bridal magazine early in my career; while I didn't know much about mortgages, I interviewed a realtor and a mortgage broker, and they gave me plenty of information for the story. I also wrote about combining two tastes into one home—a home décor story that was a great fit for a bridal magazine. In both cases, the ISG in my query letters highlighted my recent experiences of moving in together and buying my first home with my new husband.

Keep up on Trends

Although it may not seem to be, real estate and home design is a constantly changing field. "Homeowners' tastes change often and what's hot in selling/buying or remodeling now may not be the same six months from now," says Iannucci. "If you are going to write in real estate/home decorating field, then you need to keep up on the industry trades. You don't need to know exactly what fabric is what, but you should have an idea of what the latest trends are and where to find experts."

Subscribing to trade magazines that are aimed at real estate agents, builders, interior designers and residential contractors can help keep you abreast of trends. Also pay attention to what's happening where you live. Is there an increased interest in water gardens? Are more people adding on to their homes rather than moving? Have upscale condominiums become increasingly popular? Look for evidence of trends on a local level; this can provide you with story ideas as well as possible anecdotes and examples for the articles themselves.

Think Visual

Whether you're writing a piece about interior design or how to prepare your backyard garden for winter, photos, illustrations, and other art may be an integral part of the story. "Garden writing is such a visual thing," says Cathy Wilkinson Barash of Des Moines, who's been writing about gardening since 1986. "It's great to have photos that help explain it when you're suggesting a story to somebody, especially as you're starting out."

You may use photos to help sell the story idea, and then sell the photos themselves as well. Barash has honed her photography skills over the years and says that it has paid off. "You get paid more as well and often you get more for the photos than for the story itself," says Barash. Because of this, it's worth it to invest in a good-quality digital camera and take a photography class to learn the basics. And, make sure that if you are selling photos, you retain rights to them so that you resell them in the future.

Include the Human Element

For a basic how-to piece, your story may be simple in structure. For longer stories or features, you want to focus on specific details or a underlying theme that will bring your story to life. And remember that just because you're writing about interior decorating or gardening does-n't mean that you can't include a human element in your articles.

When Judy Bistany writes about design, she asks the homeowner as many questions about their lives and backgrounds as about their furniture and accessories. "I'll ask questions like, 'where have you been?' 'Where have you come from?' What do you do?'" says Bistany. She also asks who and what have influenced them throughout their lives, and incorporates that information into the story. "Then I weave the story around their personality and intermix what they've done in their home," she says. "The story is mostly about the person, while the photographic descriptions are mostly about the things."

Write Simply

If you have the ability to break down a task into simple, under-standable steps—and describe them so that someone else can follow your instructions—consider writing "how-to" articles. These stories don't require a lot of research, but they do require attention to detail. Use simple language, and make sure to point out any safety precau-tions—such as telling readers to wear goggles while using a soldering iron, for example.

Depending on the project, you may want to include photos along with your pitch to help convince the editor of your comfort level (and skill) in the subject you're pitching. Sharon Cindrich, who writes craft articles for kids, always sends mock-ups along with her pitches so edi-tors can see the finished products first-hand. Make sure that when you write the piece, you break your story into clear, easy-to-follow steps in the order readers should follow. Not sure if you've remembered every-thing? Have someone else read through your story and act it out, so you can check for missing info.

Network With Other Writers

As in other writing fields, there are several organizations aimed at journalists who cover this area. Joining one or more of them will help you get your name out as a specialist in this area and can help you nail new assignments as well. Barash is a member (and former president) of the Garden Writers Association of America as well as food writing or-ganizations, and has worked as both an editor and a freelancer. "Many of the jobs that I've gotten have been through networking," says Barash. "I moved to Des Moines to be the executive garden book editor for Meredith…and then I left that to go back to freelancing. Even the job at Meredith came through a recommendation of a fellow garden writer. It's tremendous networking."

Start Small

Writing about home and garden encompasses literally dozens of subjects, including real estate, interior decorating, garden design and maintenance, home improvement and renovations, crafts, and entertaining. If you're new to this area and want to break in, choose a subject that you have personal experience with or knowledge of and pitch some well-developed ideas to the markets you want to write for. For example, in addition to the home-related articles I wrote for bridal magazines, I could have pitched stories on buying furniture, how to choose paint colors, and a rundown on flooring options—all topics I had recent personal experience with.

Many home and garden writers get started writing for local publications to gain experience and build their clips. "For somebody who's just starting out, think local rather than universal. It can easily be worth it," says Barash. "Many regions or towns have a 'penny saver' or a local paper, some of which are syndicated over an area. If they don't have something in gardening, tell them you'd like to write for them. Have experience in gardening, especially on a local level, so you know what you're talking about. And when you don't, know who to go to."

It may be easier than you think to get these kinds of assignments. Early in my freelance career, I freelanced for a local paper, where I wrote house profiles several times a month. The stories were simple to do—I met with the realtor of a local property for sale, toured the house, and wrote a 500-word feature on the home's specifications. How did I get the work? I was already writing features for the paper, and told the feature editor there I was looking for more work. A few days later, the editor of the real estate page called and offered me a "try-out," which turned into a nice steady gig.

Pitch Seasonal Ideas

If you're writing about gardening, pitch ideas that correspond to the seasons of the year. In the spring, publications run articles about getting your garden started; during the winter, they might focus on indoor gardening topics like forcing bulbs or container gardens, for example. Scout your local community for story ideas and when you travel, be on the lookout for possible subjects. "You could do features on people who are leaders in the community doing things," says Barash. "And if there is a local horticulture society or botanic garden, be a member so you're really up on what is going on."

The same theory applies when you're writing about home-related subjects. Think about topics that tie into seasonal events. You might pitch a story on adding a backyard deck for a spring issue of a homeowners' magazine or a piece on inexpensive holiday decorating ideas for a November or December issue of a women's publication.

Develop a Specialty

Finally, consider crossover topics—stories that touch on more than one subject area—as well. For example, you might write about how to use home-grown herbs in recipes (combining food and gardening) or do a story on ways to get better bargains on antiques while traveling (a mix of interior design, money, and travel). "Look beyond the obvious topics," says Barash. "Find a niche and go for it because there are a lot of generalists out there, but if you can become known for a specific area, then people will start coming to you for information."

Barash, the author of nine books, created a unique niche for herself by starting to write about edible flowers years ago, and continues to be recognized as an authority on them. "I've become known as the expert on edible flowers," says Barash. "So, if some magazine is looking for edible flower information or a recipe or something, I'll give it to them for nothing, making sure that I'm credited as well as my book, *Edible Flowers: From Garden to Palate* (Fulcrum, 1993)."

Tales from the Front: Mary Beth Klatt

Mary Beth Klatt of Chicago has been freelancing since 1995. She's turned a long-term interest in architecture and interior design into a niche and offers this advice for writers who want to enter this area:

Follow your passions. Klatt has been fascinated with old buildings for years. When she finds one, she'll often do some research to learn about its history and architecture. If the building has an interesting story behind it, she may query it as a possible article to a publication. She's taken a similar approach with interior design stories, scouting cutting-edge homes, taking photos, and then pitching them as article subjects to her editors.

Spot trends. If you're writing about interior design, you have to keep up on the latest trends including colors, fabrics, and furniture styles. A lot of it is simply "getting out there" and paying attention to what's happening—fashion trends will often be reflected in interior design trends a few months later. "When you see the latest handbag on the street, chances are that the color will show up in your living room six months from now," says Klatt.

Network. You have to get out and meet people, says Klatt. As a relatively new design writer, she spent a lot of time at the Merchandise Mart in Chicago, where interior designers display their latest styles. She attended design seminars and introduced herself to interior designers, making valuable contacts. Now she often sets aside time to cold-call architects and designers from association websites.

Use photos. A good camera is one of the best investments you can make. "You definitely want to have scouting shots. A lot of times you can't sell the story without scouting shots because it's so visual," says Klatt. While they don't have to be expensive photos—they can be low-resolution digital shots, for example—often the photos will make or break the story.

Be accurate. If you're putting product information or shopping information in a story, it had better be correct. Double-check any information you include.

Practical Pitching:
Tips for Getting your First (or Fifteenth) Assignment

When pitching a home or garden story, your query should include the following elements:

■ An attention-getting lead, which may be anecdotal or time-oriented, such as mentioning a new decorating or real estate trend

■ Enough information about the topic so that the editor knows why the story will interest her readers

■ Details about how you will approach the piece, including the angle types of sources you plan to interview, and possible accompanying sidebars

■ An ISG that explains why you're qualified to write the piece

Take a look at the following query, which sold to *Parade*. While the writer pitched a story on real estate TV shows, the editor assigned her a piece on expert advice on "flipping" houses from the show hosts. This query is longer than usual, but it's clear from the level of detail (which came from an article the writer had already completed) that the writer is in a great position to write and report the story. Note that the writer has used a two-paragraph lead to catch the editor's attention, and given plenty of information about the story, including live quotes. Her ISG is excellent, but she could have included the section of the magazine the story is appropriate for as well as suggested word count. The bottom line is that her reporting skills and background with the subject netted her the assignment.

Dear Ms. Johnson:

Several years ago, the only television shows you could watch on buying and selling real estate were late-night or Sunday morning agonizing, yet tantalizing, infomercials touting get-rich-quick products. These shows taught viewers that by simply buying the product, purchasing property at no- or low-cost, they can reap the financial rewards of home ownership.

Fast forward a few years and the American television audience is obsessed with shows on buying, selling and redecorating their homes – just look at the proliferation of successful national television shows focusing on these topics. From Decorating on a Dime to House Hunters – where you tag along with a buyer as they review several houses and ultimately buy one – real estate television is hot.

"Buyers are becoming very clever and want hard real estate news, not just fluff," said Katrina Campins, most famous for her role as a contestant on Donald Trump's show "The Apprentice." Campins is also a top producing real estate professional and CEO of the real estate firm The Campins Company in Miami, Florida.

Campins is channeling her newly found fame and experience in the real estate industry as host of a new weekly network television real estate show, "Today in Real Estate," to be broadcast to over 1.5 million viewers in the Miami market. She hopes to nationally syndicate the show in the future.

TLC – known for such successful decorating shows as Trading Spaces – will introduce "Property Ladder," an American show based on the British show of the same name. According to a TLC spokesperson, each one-hour show will focus on a different consumer who is anxious to become a property developer. The person will purchase a property, renovate it and re-sell it – called "flipping" – hopefully making a profit. Kirsten Kemp, a designer, realtor and consultant, will host the show, providing insight as to what went wrong and right along the way. The show will debut on Saturdays in June and 12 shows will be produced this season.

According to the spokesperson, the homeowners featured on the show are footing the bill for the property and the cost of renovations and seasoned carpenters and designers won't be pitching in to help.

Will these shows still be popular in the next decade or will they disappear if the real estate market takes a down turn? "Consumers want more than get-rich quick schemes; they want to know how and where to invest," said Campins. "Real estate is a great investment and I know these shows are here to stay."

I am very interested in letting your readers know about these real estate television shows. Let me tell you a little about myself. I am a 20-year veteran of magazine and book publishing, having written articles for Shape, Parenting, Frequent Flyer, Los Angeles Times Travel Section, The Cooperator (a condo and coop monthly), and more. I write on many topics, but mostly real estate and building, remodeling and decorating. I'm also a published author of five books, including being the ghostwriter for Spectacular Homes of Florida (Panache Partners, 2006).

I am a former real estate writer for a Gannett Newspaper, writing on home remodeling, building and decorating topics. I have also written for Multi-Family Executive, Multi-Housing News and Realtor magazine.

Thank you for your time and I look forward to hearing from you soon.

Cordially,
Lisa Iannucci

The Markets: Where to Sell Home and Garden Writing

More markets cover home and garden topics than you might think. Consider these markets when looking for places to sell your work:

Shelter and gardening magazines—so-called "shelter" magazines focus on home design, décor, interior decorating, home improvement and other related subjects; gardening magazines cover a range of related topics.

General interest magazines—these magazines often cover aspects of home and gardening; angle and focus depend on the pub's readership.

Women's and men's magazines—these publications also cover a broad range of home and garden subjects. Women's magazines may focus on interior design and gardening while men's cover home improvement, remodeling and repair projects; again, every market is different.

In-flight magazines—while narrower in scope, these publications occasionally include home and garden topics, particularly design, architecture, and noteworthy gardens, buildings or other locations.

Cooking/food magazines—these publications often cover gardening subjects as well as home décor, design and entertaining.

Travel magazines—these publications often cover design, architecture, and other home-related subjects; also feature unique buildings and gardens as places to visit.

Custom publications—custom publications often cover home and garden topics because of their wide range of appeal. Stories range from do-it-yourself projects and simple garden ideas to more complex subjects; check the magazine to determine their slant and coverage.

Parenting/child care magazines—cover subjects like child-proofing your home, home decorating projects, crafts and activities to do with kids and the like.

Simplicity and nature magazines—the slant of the publication determines what subjects they cover, but these publications also cover home and garden topics as well.

National/major newspapers—cover all aspects of home and garden.

Regional/city magazines and newspapers—like their national counterparts, regional and city publications also cover a broad range of home and garden topics, many with a local angle.

Home and garden web sites—like their print versions, these markets cover a wide variety of home and garden topics. As with other online publications, stories tend to run shorter than in print markets and include quizzes, links to other sites and other interactive features.

Other Useful Stuff

Looking for sources for home or gardening articles? Consider local ones, especially if they have hands-on experience with the topic you're writing about. Below are some other organizations that may be helpful in researching these types of stories:

U.S. Botanic Garden

245 1st St. S.W.
Washington, D.C. 20024
Phone: 202-225-8333
www.usbg.gov/

Collects, cultivates and grows various plants; identifies botanic specimens and furnishes information on proper growing methods.

U.S. Department of Agriculture Resources

Floral and Nursery Plants Research Unit
3501 New York Avenue, N.E.
Room #217, Administration Building
Washington, D.C. 2002
Phone: 202-245-2726
www.usna.usda.gov/Research/

This is the research arm of the U.S. National Arboretum; includes info about gardening and plants throughout the U.S.

U.S. National Arboretum

3501 New York Avenue, N.E.
Washington, D.C. 20002
Phone: 202-245-2726
www.usna.usda.gov/

Performs research on trees, shrubs and herbaceous plants; provides info about plants/gardening.

Associations/Organizations

American Horticultural Society

7931 E. Boulevard Drive
Alexandria, VA 22308-1300
Phone: 703-768-5700 or 800-777-7931
www.ahs.org

This organization includes amateur and professional gardeners; affiliated with the American Association of Botanical Gardens and Arboreta.

American Nursery and Landscape Association
1000 Vermont Avenue NW, Suite 300
Washington, D.C. 20005-4914
Phone: 202-789-2900
www.anla.org
This 2,200-member organization includes wholesale growers, landscape firms, garden centers, mail order nurseries, and supplies.

American Society of Interior Designers
608 Massachusetts Avenue, N.E.
Washington, D.C. 20002
202-546-3480
www.interiors.org
This 38,000 member-organization is made up of practicing professional interior designers and affiliate members in allied design fields.

American Society of Landscape Architects
636 Eye Street N.W.
Washington, D.C. 20001-3736
Phone: 202-898-2444
www.asla.org
This 16,000-organization is a professional society of landscape architects.

Bio-Dynamic Farming and Gardening Association
25844 Butler Road
Junction City, OR 97448
Phone: 888-516-7797
www.biodynamics.com
Membership consists of farmers, gardeners, consumers, physicians and scientists interested in organic methods of food production.

Interior Design Society
3910 Tinsley Drive, Suite 101
High Point, NC 27265
Phone: 800-888-9590
www.interiordesignsociety.org
This organization includes retail designers, independent designers and design service firms.

National Gardening Association

1100 Dorset St.
South Burlington, VT 05403-8000
Phone: 802-863-5251
www.garden.org

This organization serves as a clearinghouse for home and community gardening information.

PLANET (Professional Lawn Care Network)

950 Herndon Parkway, Suite 450
Herndon, VA 20170
Phone: 703-736-9666 or 800-395-2522
www.plcaa.org

The association includes corporations, lawn care firms and individuals, suppliers and distributors.

Writers Associations

Garden Writers Association of America

10210 Leatherleaf Ct.
Manassas, VA 20111
Phone: 703-257-1032
www.gwaa.org

This organization consists of more than 1,800 professional newspaper and periodical garden writers, photographers, radio and television broadcasters, and book authors.

National Association of Home and Workshop Writers

C/o Dan Ramsey, President
3201 Primrose Dr.
Willits, CA 95490
Phone: 707-459-6722
www.nahww.org/

This 90-member organization consists of writers and illustrators of materials on home maintenance and improvement projects, manual skills, woodworking, and do-it-yourself projects.

Nothing but the Truth:
Writing Profiles and True-Life Features

People want to read about fascinating people. Whether it's the story of a woman who defied all odds and underwent invasive infertility treatments to have children or a harrowing tale of near-death while on a whitewater rafting trip, the public's appetite for "real life" stories is insatiable. Profiles, or pieces that introduce readers to notable people, are also popular in both consumer and trade magazines.

Writing profiles and true-life stories that capture readers' attention is an art. The writer must be able to elicit information from his subject(s) and then carefully choose what facts, stories, and insights he'll share, and in what order. Writing these types of stories also gives journalists more latitude with style. True-life dramas in particular are usually told in narrative form, similar to fiction, which offers writers the opportunity for a more creative approach than with a typical nonfiction piece.

If you've always been fascinated by people and what makes them tick, this may be a specialty for you to consider. And if you know someone who has a unique tale to tell, you may already have an "in" when it comes to pitching ideas to markets. Once you know how to locate compelling subjects, draw them out with insightful questions, and make their personalities and experiences come alive on the page, you'll be on your way to developing a lucrative niche in this area.

One of the ways to get more mileage from profile writing is to pitch your subjects to more than one magazine. For example, say one of your neighbors founded and now runs a successful nonprofit organization; in his spare time, he competes in ultramarathons. Here are several ways to spin the story:

- Pitch a profile of him to a local magazine

- Write a profile about him for his college alumni magazine

- Pitch a story on successful nonprofit entrepreneurs to a business magazine

- Write about how he balances work, home, and training for a running magazine

- Pitch a story about how to start your own nonprofit organization to a parenting magazine, using him as a source

When pitching profiles, think beyond the obvious markets, and try to come up with as many potential angles and audiences for the material as you can. That will help you maximize your time, and let you spin more than one story out of your research.

The Nuts and Bolts: How to Write Profiles and True-Life Features

Find Your Stories

The first step to writing profiles or true-life stories is simply finding the people who are the subject of the stories. What makes them worthy of an article? Have they had some extraordinary experience? Did the person face and overcome a common problem? Is she a business leader? Has he changed his community for the better? While everyone's life is interesting on some level, the person featured in a profile or a true-life story must have something unusual or unique that will capture an editor's—and eventually the readers'—attention.

Freelancer Melba Newsome of Charlotte, North Carolina has written dozens of true-life features for a variety of national magazines. She explains that while the stories may differ, they have elements in common. "Because I write these stories for women's magazines, I know the elements that they are looking for," says Newsome. "Generally, it's triumph over adversity and a story with a good ending—not necessarily a happy ending but some kind of resolution. So I look for women whose stories have those elements." She adds that her editors also say that they want the subject of the story to be "identifiable," meaning that readers should be able to relate to the person.

Make the Approach

When pitching a profile or true-life feature, you must also consider whether you'll approach your subject before you have the assignment or wait until afterwards. There are several schools of thought on this. Some writers feel that you should always approach your subject before you offer the story to confirm that he or she will participate. Other writers prefer to have the assignment in hand before they contact the person.

"I differ from a lot of people in that I don't contact my subject unless I know that someone wants the story," says Newsome. "Magazines are used to being able to not get a story they want, but the common everyday person isn't used to having a writer call them and say 'I want to tell your story' and then, having nothing happen." Because of this, Newsome usually waits to contact a possible story subject until she has a contract for the piece. "I think it carries a lot more weight with them to say 'I'm a writer and I'm on assignment for *Good Housekeeping,'* rather than saying 'I'm a writer and I don't know if anything's going to happen, but I would like to try,'" explains Newsome.

Bob Bittner of Charlotte, Michigan takes the opposite tact. "I like to touch base with the person, especially if I get my initial idea say, from a newspaper story," he says. "I want to be sure that the newspaper writer that I am basing my pitch on got the details right so I want to talk to the person and at least let him or her know what's in the works. I don't mention specific publications by name and I don't in any way want them to assume that it's a done deal or that the story would be limited to one publication. I like to have the flexibility to take that story and run with it in as many ways as possible."

Track Them Down

Depending on the story, you may already know the person you're writing about or he or she may be relatively easy to locate. In other cases, you may hear about a person and then have to track him or her down using the Internet and other sources. Newsome reads about possible story subjects in the local paper or sees them on talk television shows, which often mention where they live. She then uses the phone book and the Internet to locate her sources. (There are dozens of search engines and Internet directories for this purpose—see "Other Useful Stuff" at the end of the chapter for more information about them.)

A few quick tips on searching: while search engines vary in terms of how they operate, I've had the most success locating people with sites like www.google.com. Try putting in different combinations of the person's name and/or other information you have about them—a city, state, profession, or other criteria. Internet telephone directories can also be helpful, but the information in them can be out of date. And if you're looking for someone with a fairly common name, you may get too many hits to follow up on. Don't forget to ask your reference librarian if she has any suggestions as well.

Get the Details

When interviewing and researching the story, make sure to nail down details and specific facts. Taping interviews will help protect you if a subject says something and then tries to recant it later, but ask people for permission to tape before you do so.

During interviews for a true-life feature story, ask plenty of detail-oriented questions so that you'll be able to accurately reprise the story. Ask questions that involve all five senses—sight, sound, touch, taste and smell. You want to be able to paint a picture with your story, so be prepared to spend lots of time getting background information.

Depending on the story, you may ask things like "what were you wearing that afternoon?" "What first attracted you to your husband?" "What did your mother say when you told her you had cancer?" If you're asking about emotionally charged experiences, be prepared to take your time and allow your subject plenty of time to answer and respond.

Do Your Homework

With some types of profiles, your background research may be minimal. But if you're interviewing someone who's well-known in his or her field or is notable in some way, you should prepare in advance. "Depending on the type of person you're going to interview, you're likely to try to find some old publicity clips that mention this person. If the person has a publicist or is an executive of an organization or company, you'll likely get some handouts about the interviewee's background," says freelancer Sal Caputo of Tempe, Arizona, who writes profiles and covers music, business, and entertainment subjects as well. "If this profile is an extensive one, then just as you would for any other feature or news story, you're going to want to identify sources you can talk to who can help you understand the subject." While you may only use those interviews as background, you'll also want to verify any information you come across with your subject or through other sources.

"I think it's important to do at least a moderate amount [of preparation] because it really irritates the person who you're interviewing if there are key things about them that you don't know," agrees Susanne Alexander, a freelancer from Cleveland, Ohio who writes profiles as well as business and health pieces. "It can really break down the interview if you come across as being uninformed about them."

Ask the Right Questions—and Establish a Rapport

When it comes to the actual interview, your approach may depend on whether the person has been interviewed before. For example, if you're doing a profile, you don't want to cover a lot of the same ground with the person. "Ask yourself why you're doing the profile and whether other profiles have been done on this person," says Caputo. "This will help you to know what's commonly known about the person, so that you can ask questions that probe a little more deeply. In the interview, though, always assume that all your research is wrong. As much as you can, quickly verify with the profile subject the truth of the main points you want to make as a result of your research, and get the subject to elaborate on your key points if possible."

When conducting interviews, there is always a give and take involved. For profiles and true-life stories, it's even more important for the interviewee to feel comfortable. One way to do that is to look for ways to connect with the person at the outset of the interview, but you have to be sensitive to the person's response, says Alexander. "There are times when, in an effort to build relatedness, I might share something personal with myself or an experience that connects in some way with what they're talking about. Then I listen very carefully to how they respond," says Alexander. "If I get very little or no response back then I won't do that again for the rest of the call."

Get a Sense of the Person

For longer profiles and true-life stories, it's preferable to conduct your interviews in person. "You get a sense from their facial expressions as to what's important to them and whether they're being straight with you or not," says Alexander. "You can see their mannerisms and expressions and get a much better feel for what they're enthusiastic about and what they feel strongly about."

Another advantage is that if you meet your subject at home or at work, you're given additional clues to his or her character. "You also definitely get a sense from their environment about what's important to them," says Alexander. "Do they have family pictures up? Do they have fishing trophies up? If I'm doing the interview by phone, I'll ask them to describe their environment to me and say something like 'tell me what's around you, tell me what the setting's like.'" Those details—and the explanations behind them—can help flesh out a story.

Ask questions that go beyond the typical "what has been your greatest business success" or "would you do anything differently if you had your life to live over?" "I always try to come up with questions that go to their heart, not necessarily what they've done but why they've done something," says Alexander. "You want people get a real sense of what's important to them as a person as opposed as to the surface level of their life."

Listen up

While it's helpful to have an outline or list of questions you want to ask, it's often beneficial to stray from that list occasionally. "The writer must ask all the pertinent questions and ensure the accuracy of the answers. But, a good interviewer is also willing to veer off the subject, if a more engaging one surfaces and so begins the act of balancing," says freelancer and former magazine editor Kelly Boyer Sagert of Lorain, Ohio. "My personal solution is this: I research the subject of the interview and jot down thoughts in preparation, but I never create a hard and fast set of questions. I want my interviews to have the flavor of a pleasant yet professional conversation.

"While you're interviewing, the thing I've learned is not to be so set in your ways that you miss an extraordinary story," says Sagert. "Like, if you ask a question and they say 'oh by the way, I committed a horrible crime' and you go on with 'so, where did you go to high school?'" Sagert once profiled a retired photographer who donated his time to the local cable television station—a fairly simple piece. At the conclusion of the interview, she asked him about his accent.

It turned out that the photographer had been born in Hungary to millionaire parents and grown up in a mansion with dozens of servants—until the Nazis arrived in Hungary and put his family in a concentration camp. His mother died there and he and his father came to the United States. When his father broke his back, the teenaged boy was forced to find a job and photography was all he knew. "I asked him, 'Can I tell this story?'" says Sagert. "And he said, 'Yeah, if you think anyone cares!'" One off-hand question led to a remarkable profile.

Finally, include a general, open-ended question at the conclusion of the interview, says Caputo. "Always ask whether there is something else that you haven't touched upon that they wish to mention," says Caputo. "Quite often, they have nothing, but every now and again, this question turns up brand-new information that the interview subject, now comfortable with you, would never have mentioned earlier."

Pick a Point of View

When telling a true-life feature, you have to choose whether you'll tell the piece in third person or in first person, also called an "as-told-to." There are advantages and drawbacks with each approach. If you tell the piece in third person, you have more latitude and can share more information. A first-person story may be more gripping but it will also limit what you can include.

For example, when Newsome wrote a first-person story about a woman who was stranded in the Alaskan wilderness, she could only share the woman's personal experience—she couldn't talk about the rescue parties that were searching for her or share other information the way she could have in a third-person piece. But for that story, she wanted readers to have a sense of what the woman was going through and her fear that she might not ever be found. Choosing to tell her story in the first person brought those emotions out more convincingly than a third-person piece.

Pull it Together

Writing the true-life story requires reviewing your interviews and research to determine which moments you want to illuminate in your piece. "The most important thing to remember is when you're interviewing the person, listen for those moments where it tugs at your heart," says Newsome. "When I interview someone, the part that strikes me is the part that strikes the reader. Focus in on those parts that have the drama and be sure be sure to tell that."

Like fiction, true-life stories usually follow a linear form with a beginning, middle and end. You want to give enough background so that the readers will care about the people involved, tell the story, and finally have a resolution.

When writing profiles, you'll want a mix of running text and quotes from your subject and possibly quotes from others as well. "It's a balancing act between narrative and quotes," says Sagert. "I try to separate what should be quotes and what should be narrative, and pull out the strongest quotes and best words."

With profiles, you want to go beyond simply sharing details about your subject's life—you want conflict and resolution, says Caputo. "If this person has made some dramatic achievement, what obstacles did he or she overcome? If the person was on the fast track all his or her life, it's going to be a pretty dull story, but everybody has setbacks or qualms or phobias," he says. "These points of weakness or stress (a businessman who decides he wants to be top dog but also wants to give his family plenty of time and so has to juggle even greater demands than the guy who just puts his family on the back burner) or contradiction and complexity (the producer of a risqué show that's on in prime time who doesn't let his children watch TV because it's too risqué) are what you want to illuminate."

Tales from the Front: Kristin Baird Rattini

Freelancer Kristin Baird Rattini of Howell, New Jersey,, has written more than 200 profiles as a freelancer for trade and consumer magazines and newspapers. She offers these tips for writers who are new to writing profiles:

Don't talk too much. "There's a fine line. You have to establish a conversation; when it seems more like a conversation instead of an interview, subjects tend to open up more," says Rattini. "But you have to stop yourself from talking too much. This story is about the subject; it's their voice you want to hear, their story you're trying to tell. So zip your lip, and simply listen."

Remember the simple courtesies, especially respecting your subject's time. Always confirm that this is a convenient time to talk. And always call on time. Rattini was recently thanked profusely by a subject for calling on time. He told her he's interviewed frequently, and how other writers have called as much as a half-hour or hour late with no explanation. He was impressed with her punctuality and professionalism, and gave a much more gregarious interview than she might otherwise have expected.

Get under the surface. "Personal profiles are a format where it's easy to fall into cliché," warns Rattini. "The hero. The martyr. The underdog. While that tagline is often what sells the piece, it will sink the piece if you don't flesh out your subject beyond that label." Dig deep during your interviews so that you can present a well-rounded story rather than a one-dimensional look at someone.

Think outside the box. If your subject's someone who is frequently interviewed, they've developed pat answers that they have at the ready for when those inevitable questions arise. Surprise your subject by asking questions that will jolt them out of their rut. "When I interviewed Jim Davis [the cartoonist who writes the Garfield strip] for *Boys' Life*, I read several previous interviews he'd given," says Rattini. "I saw several answers repeated from one story to another. I took great care to avoid those ruts. Since I was also interviewing 'Garfield,' I played to Garfield's attitude, knowing he would rise to the occasion. Several times during my interview, after hearing my question, Davis' first response was, "Great question. I've never thought about that one before.""

Practical Pitching:
Tips for Getting your First (or Fifteenth) Assignment

When pitching a profile or true-life feature, your query should include the following elements:

■ An attention-getting lead, which introduces the person to be profiled or provides the "hook" of the story

■ Enough information about the person or true-life story so that the editor knows why the piece will interest her readers

■ Details about how you will approach the piece

■ An ISG that explains why you're qualified to write the piece

Take a look at the following profile query, which sold to *Family Circle*. Note the amount of detail the writer has provided about the Butterfly Lady—it's clear that he has already interviewed her (and in fact had met her in person.) In addition, the query does an excellent job of capturing what makes the subject interesting and unique, including live quotes that give the editor a sense of the subject's personality and outlook. Finally, the writer has demonstrated an excellent ISG—he's already met the Butterfly Lady, and he's written other profiles as well. Even if he hadn't, his query shows his writing skill, which should easily convince an editor to give him the assignment.

Chandra: I hope the following idea will be just what you're looking for in a "Passions" story. I'd love to write it for you.

QUERY: The Butterfly Lady

Deborah Payne smiles as she mentions the comments that greeted her four children after the family opened their new ranch in the Texas Hill Country. "The first couple of weeks, they heard a lot of jokes like 'Bet those herds are pretty hard to lasso!' and 'Isn't it kind of hard to keep them in the corral?' It didn't take too long for that to get old," she says, laughing. Of course, she should have expected it. After all, this part of the country is known for its cattle and horses and the occasional llama. The last thing you'd expect to find is a rancher whose herds flock and flutter. But, then, the Fredericksburg Butterfly Ranch and Habitat isn't a typical Texas ranch.

Owner Deborah Payne, 43, is the person primarily responsible for the new company's success. While a growing number of butterfly-farm competitors focus solely on mail-order business, Deborah is an enthusiastic educator and curator who thrives on visitors. "Our mission," she says, "is to promote and encourage the creation of backyard habitats to help increase butterflies' natural population." She urges guests to spend time relaxing in the landscaped butterfly habitat of water fountains and plant varieties that provide nectar and food for her colorful herds. She leads the curious on tours of her new 1,500-square-foot walk-through butterfly house, a temperature-controlled environment where orange-black clouds of adult Monarchs and Painted Ladies flutter past. Armed with a wealth of knowledge and a passion for her work, Deborah is like a park ranger who can hold the wonders of her natural world — eggs, chrysalises, caterpillars — in the palm of her hand.

"I had sat at home for 13 years, raising the kids," says Deborah. "But I just got to the point where I wanted to do something. I knew I wanted to be outside and that I wanted to involve the kids. I grew up on a farm and wanted the same kind of lifestyle for my family. Then I saw an article where a Texas woman talked about raising butterflies and the positive effects butterflies have had on people throughout history. So I took one of her seminars to learn more about how to raise butterflies on my own. After more than six months of reading, research, and information gathering, I raised my first butterflies in our utility room at home. At one point, there were a thousand monarch caterpillars in there! When they would eat at night, it was like a roar with all of their chomping. After that, the business side of things just took off." But why butterflies? "For a lot of cultures throughout history, butterflies have symbolized spirit and the inner being," Deborah explains. "Nowadays, people release them at weddings to symbolize promises and prayers for the future. And people release them at memorial services to represent the soul of their loved one rising to heaven. And, of course, they're beautiful and they help with pollination."

Since launching her business in mid-1999, she has turned a fascination with butterflies into a thriving business with a growing, national reputation. She now raises 12 butterfly species that she sells for release at weddings, memorial services, and other special events. In addition, she has integrated her family life with her business, creating a nurturing and stimulating world for her butterflies as well as for her husband, Perry, and young children Tara, Will, Laura, and Kristen.

In addition to the recent "Passions" piece about castle fan Linda Mueller that I wrote for you, my articles have sold to a wide variety of publications, including Family Circle, Working Mother, Preservation, Pages, and The Writer.

I think your readers would enjoy discovering Deborah's passion. I hope you'll agree — and that we'll be talking soon about an assignment. Thanks so much for your consideration.

Take care,
Bob

Markets: Where to Sell Profiles and True-Life Features

There's no shortage of markets for profiles and true-life features ranging from small local publications to national glossies. Nearly every publication features some sort of profiles; keep the market in mind when you pitch potential story subjects whether it's a simple profile or a dramatic true-life story.

Some of the biggest markets for profiles and true-life features include:

General interest magazines—include profiles of business and political leaders, innovators, athletes, other people of note; also publish newsy stories and true-life features.

Professional and trade journals—use a lot of profiles of successful people in their respective businesses and industries.

Women's and men's magazines—these magazines profile people who have accomplished something newsworthy, whether they're sports figures, celebrities, or "real people" who have experienced something unusual.

Parenting magazines—include more true-life features but may include profiles as well, depending on the magazine.

In-flight publications—often include profiles of successful business executives, analysts and pundits, "movers and shakers," celebrities, and other notables.

National/major newspapers—include a broad range of profiles such as business leaders, sports figures, celebrities, and the like; also include true-life feature stories.

Regional/city magazines and newspapers—like their national counterparts, regional and city publications also include a broad range of profiles of notable local residents and true-life features.

Other Useful Stuff

To write compelling profiles and true-life features, you need excellent interviewing skills and a genuine interest in the people you're speaking to and writing about. You may also have to use the Internet and other sources to locate potential story subjects. Listed below are several internet resources and books that may be helpful for freelancers who want to write profiles and true-life features:

Internet Telephone Directories

While there are dozens to choose from, the following are my favorites:

www.anywho.com

www.bigfoot.com
www.switchboard.com

Books

Creative Interviewing: The Writer's Guide to Gathering Information by Asking Questions, 3rd Edition, by Ken Metzler (Allyn & Bacon, 1997); overview of interviewing techniques including ways to overcome "interview anxiety," get subjects to open up, and write profiles.

Feminine Wiles: Creative Techniques for Writing Women's Feature Stories that Sell, by Donna Elizabeth Boetig (Quill Driver Books, 1998); practical suggestions and examples for selling to the women's magazine market.

Writing for Story, by Jon Franklin (Penquin Group, 1994); practical advice on feature writing including information-gathering, structure, and editing.

Section Three: Growing Your Writing Business

Broaden Your Horizons: Branching Out

While this book focuses on writing and selling nonfiction articles, at some point, you may want to expand your writing career into other areas. Do you want to write books? Interested in picking up corporate work? Or maybe you'd like to consult, speak, or develop a web-based business. As a freelancer, there's no specific career track to follow—the path you choose is entirely of your own making.

When you specialize, however, you're better positioned to take advantage of other opportunities. You've already developed an expertise in one or more subjects, which sets you apart from other writers. You can easily use that knowledge to branch into related fields including book authorship, speaking, and consulting.

While there are a variety of lucrative gigs available for talented writers, this chapter includes a brief look at some of the most popular. Read on for more information about some of the ways you can diversify your writing career and continue to build your platform.

Contributing Editor

You've probably seen names and "Contributing Editor" ("CE") on the mastheads of some of your favorite magazines. Usually this means that the CE is a writer who has an ongoing relationship with the publication. He or she may have been a former fulltime staffer or a freelancer; in any case, the writer produces stories for the publication on a regular basis.

Some contributing editors have an agreement to write a certain number of stories for a certain amount of money each month; some write as many pieces as the editor needs for that issue; and others receive a retainer regardless of what they produce that month. As a freelancer, it's worth it to seek out CE gigs—they offer steady income and the opportunity to develop long-lasting relationships with publications. As a specialist, you're in a great position to obtain CE gigs, and having your name on the masthead can lead to other writing assignments as well.

Margaret Littman, a freelancer based in Chicago, has had a number of contributing editor jobs, including at *Crain's Chicago Business, Teen, Snack Food Magazine, Bakery Production,* and *Marketing* during her freelance career. How did she get them? She simply asked. "I make sure it is an editor I feel appreciates me and someone with whom I want to work on a more regular basis," says Littman, who's currently at CE at *Chain Leader,* a trade magazine. "If I get a vibe that they're really appreciative of what I do…I've asked to make it more formal."

Littman agrees that there are several advantages to being a CE. They often make more money than "standard" freelancers—some magazines have paid her a flat monthly retainer in addition to what she gets for the stories she writes. As a CE, she also knows that she'll be receiving a check at the same time every month, which makes managing her cash flow a little easier.

Another aspect Littman, a former magazine editor, enjoys is the chance to work more closely with the editors on stories. "It's not just querying and then waiting to see if they accept it," says the former magazine editor. "I feel like I have a little more say in shaping the stories, and shaping the section or direction they take. I like that—for me, it's a good compromise. I don't miss editing on a day-to-day basis, but as a freelancer I do sometimes miss the big picture editing in terms of thinking and developing a whole package for a story."

If you're going to approach a market about becoming a CE, you should already have a good relationship with the publication. Consider the benefits to the magazine of making you a CE so that you can make a strong argument in your favor. "Think about why the editor would want to do this as opposed to why you want it," says Littman. Point out that as a contributing editor, you'll always be available for assignments, which will save them time and hassle looking for other writers. If you'll come up with ideas for the editors, show how this will benefit her as well. "If you have an agreement where you're going to come up with the ideas or maybe 50 percent of the ideas that you're writing, that's another time saver for them," says Littman. "Point out why it's good for them."

Another plus? While there are no guarantees, contributing editor jobs also tend to be a little more stable than simply freelancing for a magazine. "You have some job security," says Littman. "If they have to cut back, they'll give something to me before they give something to another freelancer." The one drawback is that as a CE, the magazine you work for may ask you not to write for any of its competitors. That's the possible tradeoff to the relationship, but for most writers, it's worth it.

Book Author

It's not surprising that many nonfiction writers start with magazine articles and continue on into books. While books take much longer to produce, royalties can provide additional income for years—although some authors write books for a specific sum in exchange for the copyright rather than for an advance and potential royalties.

An idea for a nonfiction book is a great place to begin, but an idea isn't enough. To become a book author, you must also have what publishing pros call "platform." Platform is what you bring to a book in terms of your expertise, your reputation, your media connections, your audience—in short, how well-known you are and how many people you can convince to buy the book.

That's where specializing helps once again. Melanie Bowden, a parenting writer, recently published her first book, *Why Didn't Anyone Tell me That? True Stories of New Motherhood* (First Books, 2006.) Kelly Boyer Sagert's profile-writing work helped her land her first book deal, *Joe Jackson: A Biography* (Greenwood Press, 2004); she's currently working on her third book. Josh Karp, who has written profiles and business stories, saw his first book, *A Futile and Stupid Gesture: How Doug Kenney and National Lampoon Changed Comedy Forever* (Chicago Review Press, 2006) published in the fall of 2006.

Specializing in a subject helps you create a platform as you become an expert in your subject area. The other way to develop a platform is to become a celebrity of sorts, or to get as close to a celebrity as you can. Consider Dr. Phil McGraw. He was a moderately successful "life strategist" who became a household name after he started appearing on Oprah's daytime talk show. His own series soon followed, and now even his wife and son are best-selling authors.

Or your life experience may give you platform, as it did with Amber Frey, who had an affair with convicted murdered Scott Peterson. Her publisher, Regan Books, knew that people would want to read her story, and she got a sizable advance for her book, *Witness: For the Prosecution of Scott Peterson.*

However, most of us don't have celebrity connections or compelling melodramatic stories to share. That means you have to develop your platform on your own—in other words, specializing. The next step is writing a book proposal. Nine out of 10 nonfiction books are sold on the basis of a book proposal, rather than a finished manuscript. The proposal should convince a publisher that the book will sell enough copies for it to make a profit. It will also help you research and organize your material before you begin the book itself.

While the format of book proposals varies, most include the following elements:

An overview, which summarizes the concept and your background as the author

A description of the audience for the book

An "about the author" section where you highlight your relevant experience and unique expertise that qualifies you to write the book

A marketing and promotion section that explains how you plan to sell the book

A competition analysis, which lists books similar to yours and distinguishes yours from the competition in a positive way

An outline of the book itself, including chapter summaries

At least one sample chapter

Let's look at each of these elements in turn. First, the overview is a page or two at the beginning of the proposal, designed to grab the editor's attention, make the case for the book, and compel her to read the rest of the proposal.

The audience section describes the potential market for the book; and you can't claim that your book will be aimed at "anyone and everyone." Who will the book appeal to? History buffs? Busy parents trying to get their children to eat better? First-time home builders? Would-be EBay.com millionaires? As the author, you should be able to describe your target audience in the proposal, and use statistics if you can—for example, "this book is aimed at the 1.7 million active U.S. military personnel."

Don't be shy in the "about the author" section. Sing your praises, and highlight the experience that makes you the perfect person to write this book. For example, when I pitched my first book—which happens to be the one you're reading!—I described how I'd built a successful freelance career by specializing in health, fitness, and nutrition subjects. I also noted my significant magazine-writing experience, my experience teaching and leading writing workshops, and the fact that I had published articles in a variety of writing magazines. In a word, that's platform, and that's what your "about the author" section should include.

The author section may naturally segue into the marketing and promotion section. Spend plenty of time here demonstrating how you'll sell the title, and go beyond bookstore events. Will you launch your own media campaign? Promote the title through a specially-designed website and newsletter? Partner with a company or association to market the book? The more yo"re willing and able to do to promote your title, the better. Publishers want authors who will go out and sell, sell, sell.

Mention the competition, and show how your book will differ (and hopefully be better than) others on the same subject. Finally, the chapter summaries and sample chapters show the editor what your book will contain, and showcase your writing style.

Make Your Pitch

When making your initial pitch, most editors and agents want to see a query letter rather than the full proposal. This query is similar to a magazine article query; you'll want to catch the editor's attention, describe what makes your book unique, demonstrate the market for it, and mention your relevant qualifications. If you can, demonstrate familiarity with the agent or editor's work by mentioning a book he or she has published or represented. Here's an example:

July 21, 2000

Laurie Harper
The Sebastian Agency
172 East Sixth Street, Suite 2005
St. Paul, Minnesota 55101

Dear Ms. Harper:

I've heard good things about you from fellow ASJA member Tina Tessina and am writing to query you about a nonfiction book proposal you may be interested in:

Falling in love is the easy part—it's the day-to-day challenges that really put a relationship to the test. But while maintaining a strong, loving bond is difficult for even the most committed couples, those in long-distance relationships face an even greater challenge.

According to recent statistics, at least 1 million Americans currently have commuter marriages and maintain two separate households. Millions more—including the more than 1,300,000 men and women in the U.S. armed services—face extended time away from each other because of jobs that require frequent travel. And every fall as students leave to attend college and graduate school, hundreds of thousands of dating and engaged couples face the prospect of long-distance love as well.

Any couple faced with a long-distance relationship faces a multitude of concerns. Will distance threaten their relationship? How will they maintain intimacy? What kind of financial burden will it cause? How will it affect the couple's future? Is infidelity more likely? What if children are involved? How do they know if this is the right decision? How will they cope with the inevitable stress of being apart?

My book, Make the Heart Grow Fonder: How to Survive—and Thrive in—Your Long-Distance Relationship will answer all of the questions and concerns that these couples face. Heart will include the experiences of hundreds of long-distance relationship "veterans" as well as expert advice from psychologists and relationship experts. The book will also feature quizzes and activities for couples to use to determine whether a long-distance relationship is a healthy option for their relationship as well as ways to cope with loneliness and separation, tips on dealing with the financial burden these relationships can cause, and advice for parents who want to maintain a close relationship with their children regardless of physical distance. Heart will also look at the reasons for the growing trend in long-distance relationships and report on recent research on the factors that influence the success and stability of such relationships.

This down-to-earth, anecdote-filled book will be both a source of strength and encouragement as well as a wealth of practical information for the millions of people facing this increasingly common challenge. As a fulltime freelance journalist and a veteran of three long-distance relationships, I can bring a unique perspective to this timely subject.

I hope you'll be interested in reviewing my book proposal for Heart—please let me know if I may send it to you immediately. Thank you very much for your time; I look forward to hearing from you soon.

Very truly yours,
Kelly James-Enger

Note that this query explains why I'm contacting her, briefly describes the idea behind the book and proves there's a market for it with relevant statistics. It also explains what the book will includes, and summarizes my qualifications to write it.

Agent versus Editor

The sample query letter was aimed at an agent (and in fact nabbed me my agent years ago.) Which brings up the question of agents—as in, do you need one, and how do you get one?

No, you don't have to have an agent to sell your book—you can approach editors on your own. But an agent is likely to know much more about the world of publishing (as in what editors are buying, and for how much) than you do. He's up on trends, has a feel for what editors are looking for, and has experience negotiating and working with publishers.

How do you find an agent? Same place you find editors, by starting with a market guide like *Jeff Herman's Guide to Book Publishers, Editors, and Literary Agents 2007* (Three Dog Books, 2006) or *Writer's Market 2007* (Writer's Digest, 2006), and making a master list of possible agents who represent your type of book. Consider how long the agent has been in business, the size of his agency, and the authors he represents. Today the vast majority of agents have their own websites, where they post their writers' guidelines, authors they represent, and information about their agencies. You may also meet agents at writers' conferences, or receive recommendations from other writers you know.

In addition, I recommend visiting the bookstore to look for books that are similar in topic or approach to your own. In the "Acknowledgements" section, you'll often find the name of the agent of the book—authors like to thank their agent and editor by name. Add those agents to your list. After you've researched the possibilities and narrowed the field down to your top choices, send query letters out to your top picks. Any agent who wants to see more will ask for your proposal (in the case of nonfiction) or complete manuscript (with fiction).

If an agent wants to represent you, the industry standard fee is 15 percent, which means that your agent takes a cut of every book deal he or she negotiates for you. (If your book doesn't sell, however, your agent doesn't collect anything. A reputable agent will never charge for "reading fees," for example—he gets paid when you get paid.) Your agent will then shop your proposal around, hopefully selling your book and negotiating a great deal for you with the publisher. If you choose to work alone, you'll work as your own agent, contacting editors yourself.

Corporate Writer

One of the most lucrative writing areas for freelancers is writing for corporations or businesses. (By this I mean writing for corporations, not about them as with articles about business or corporations.) The work isn't always glamorous or interesting, but the pay often makes it worthwhile.

When freelancer Polly Campbell of Beaverton, Oregon, started her own PR and freelance business, she did a lot of work for local businesses. "Corporate writing really draws on your writing skills and your ability to connect with people through words," says Campbell. "It's not about creating something that's a part of you as much as it is creating something that services the client. So you have to always understand the mission at hand and what they're trying to convey, and then figure out a way to diplomatically tell them which style is going to work for them effectively."

If you're interested in writing for corporations, the first step is finding clients. "You have to be in areas where those people are going to go, and you need to dress like them, and think like a business person," says Campbell. "When I was focused on corporate writing, I was at the chamber meetings and doing the network lunches. That was the commitment I made and it paid off. You don't go to those things in jeans and a sweater; you go in a suit. You need to be on the corporate level with them."

Writers who work for corporations (we'll call them "copywriters," although most write more than ad copy) often charge hourly rates of $50 to $100, depending on their market or expertise, or they charge by the project. When you're starting out in this niche, you probably can't charge as much as more experienced copywriters, but be careful not to undersell yourself either, especially if you already have a background in the subject area. Depending on where you're located, $40-$60/hour may be a fair rate.

If you have a business background, that's great, but if not, educate yourself about sales writing techniques. When writing ad copy, for example, you should know the difference between features and benefits (for the record, features are aspects of a company's product or service while benefits are how they impact the customers' lives.) Robert Bly has some excellent books on copywriting, including *Secrets of a Freelance Writer: How to Make $85,000 a Year* (Henry Holt, 1997), which address the basics of writing pieces like brochures, ads, and sales letters.

Making Your Approach

The next step is finding clients, which may be easier than you think. Make a list of area companies you can contact, and spread the word that you're available for copywriting projects. If you don't have any samples to show, offer to write brochures, newsletters or ads for your favorite non-profit organization to make contacts and develop your portfolio.

While it may be nerve-wracking at first, cold calls are the most efficient way to contact companies about writing projects. Introduce yourself, and ask if the person at the company has a need for a writer. Try to make an appointment for a face-to-face meeting where you can bring your portfolio. If your contact asks for more information, send a letter along with a few samples of your work, and then follow up on the package a few weeks later.

What Corporations Want

Writing for businesses requires many of the same skills as writing for a magazine or book publisher. You're expected to turn in well-written work on deadline, and to behave professionally. If you've been used to working with hands-on editors, however, writing for corporate clients can be an eye-opener. Most expect you to come in, gather the information you need, and produce clean, professional-looking copy the first time out.

Being able to grasp the nature of the company, the motive behind the project you're working on, and the corporate culture is an essential part of copywriting. Just as you'd keep a publication's readership in mind when writing a magazine article, you must also keep the customers or corporate audience in mind while writing for a business. For example, when I was hired to write newsletters for The Pampered Chef, I asked about the typical Kitchen Consultants who would be reading them so I had a good feel for the audience. That kind of understanding is what makes you invaluable to corporations, and can help ensure a steady flow of work. As your portfolio and experience grow, you can step up to the next level, working for larger corporations and raising your fees.

Speaker

Not every writer enjoys the thought of standing at a podium before an audience. For those who do—and have a platform as well as natural speaking skills—speaking can be a lucrative sideline. Ed Gordon, an author, freelance writer and speaker from Chicago, has turned his business and educational expertise into a successful speaking career. "A lot of writers are shy and don't have the skill set [to be a successful speaker]," says Gordon. "But a lot of speakers don't have any content, so I fill a very useful niche."

Gordon developed his speaking talent over many years, and suggests that writers who are interested in this field hone their presentation skills. "You have to learn how to become a professional speaker," says Gordon. "If you don't have opportunities to give public presentations now, you have to get them and you have to develop those skills. Join Toastmasters, join volunteer organizations and volunteer to give presentations. You can also join a group like National Speakers Association." While content is important, you can also improve your voice tone, your ability to project your voice, and master other mechanics of speaking.

Consider what your "platform," or specialty, will be and how you'll use this to market yourself. "That's where journalists have a tremendous advantage," says Gordon. "They have content and they've done a lot of research already. If you want to be a professional speaker, you have to be an expert in something. The value of journalists doing this is that many are experts in a particular area and they've published. Even if they only have articles written, they're good handouts for a program."

A good way to hone your speaking skills is to teach a noncredit class at your local community college. I started teaching magazine-writing classes early in my career, and then branched out to speaking at writers' conferences and libraries. While I had limited myself to writing-related topics, I realized my background in health and fitness gave me the background I needed to speak about wellness subjects as well. Now I speak on topics like stress management, time management, and healthy habits, to a variety of audiences. Specializing has given me an expertise that I can use to obtain speaking gigs—and an opportunity to sell books to attendees as well.

Consultant

Another way to get paid for the body of knowledge you've developed is to consult. Tom Brosnahan, a fulltime travel freelancer based in Concord, Massachusetts, performs itinerary planning, on-the-ground guidance (like leading a Discovery Channel scouting team around Turkey looking for filming locations), guidebook author recruitment, and other services for clients.

"Anyone with expertise can act as a consultant; anyone who has written a book or lots of articles on the same topic is an expert (to most of the world)," says Brosnahan. "Your expertise is the important thing, but the way you sell yourself is what actually gets you an income from your expertise."

To be a successful consultant, you can't be bashful. "If you know your stuff, act that way and potential clients will take you at your word and pay accordingly," says Brosnahan. He suggests consultants do the following:

■ Set up a different persona for yourself as "expert consultant" as opposed to your identity as a writer

■ Describe your expertise and its usefulness accurately and in detail

■ Create professional business cards and letterhead (in addition to the ones you already use for your writing business)

■ Market your services whenever you have the opportunity

■ Put up a simple web page as an internet calling card

■ Work out a rate schedule so you know what to charge when someone asks

Also, be sure to set your prices high enough. "If someone really needs the expertise you have, it means you can solve a problem for them. They are willing to pay good money for this," says Brosnahan. "A decent starting rate is $100 per hour, plus expenses. (Professional consultants with first-rate business credentials earn $1,500 to $2,000 per day and up!)"

Decide in advance whether you will bill by the hour, half-hour, quarter-hour or minute; whether you will require a time minimum (like two hours or a half-day, for example) and whether you will charge for time spent traveling. And be ready to write a detailed proposal with an estimated total fee for larger projects or to answer questions from potential clients. As a specialist, you know far more about a subject or two than most people do. Consulting lets you charge for that knowledge and expertise, and it can lead to other work as well.

Content Provider

This is just a fancy name for selling reprint rights to your work. Many writers ignore reprint possibilities and focus only on original assignments. That's a mistake, especially when you specialize. Most reprint markets don't pay as well as national consumer magazines do, but even small checks can add up quickly. Think of yourself as a content provider and you can get paid more than once for the stories you've already researched and written.

Not convinced? Last year, I made more than $10,000 from selling reprint rights, and this year I'm on target to hit that number again. Here's how you can turn your finished articles into additional checks.

Read Your Contracts Carefully

Obviously you can only resell work that you own the rights to. If you sign an all-rights contract, you can't offer reprint rights to that story to another market. (You can always write about the topic again for a new market, but that's an entirely new story, not a reprint of your original piece.) Other contracts provide exclusivity provisions which may preclude you from selling reprint rights for a certain time period or to a certain type of magazine.

Even when an all-rights contract is forced on me, I always try to negotiate so that I retain rights to my articles; I've had publishers (albeit grudgingly) agree to that. Sure, the publisher is still going to do whatever it wants with my work for no extra money—but at least I'm free to resell it on my own if I want to.

Locate Reprint Markets

Now comes the time-consuming part—actually finding markets for your work. I've found my most lucrative markets the old-fashioned way—by legwork. When I travel, I always look at local newsstands for magazines that may be interested in my work. Smaller, regional, and special-interest magazines are all possibilities. While market guides like *Writer's Market* will list markets that buy reprint rights, there's no substitute for simply looking on your own. Check out publication directories like *The Standard Periodical Directory* (your local library should have it on reserve) for a more comprehensive list of potential markets. And don't forget to ask your friends (especially non-writers!) to save magazines for you.

Maximize Your Sales

Here's the thing: I don't bother selling one story at a time. I'm a content provider, remember? Because I specialize, I have a slew of stories in broad general areas like health, fitness, nutrition, and relationships and weddings. Rather than sending out one story to a potential reprint market, I send a cover letter and list of story titles and topics—it's often just as easy to sell three or four stories at once rather than just one.

I always customize my initial contact letter to match the magazine I'm pitching. Here's what an initial contact letter to a regional bridal magazine looks like:

Dear Ms. Smith:

I'm a full-time freelance journalist whose work has appeared in more than 50 national magazines including BRIDE'S, Bridal Guide, For the Bride, Wedding Bells, Fitness, Fit, Shape, Redbook, Woman's Day, Family Circle, and Marie Claire. Over the past years, I've developed an inventory of "evergreen" bridal stories which I offer to regional bridal markets like yours that looking for well-written, informative articles for their readers. Currently I have stories on the following topics available (approximate word count is shown as well):

"50 Health and Fitness Tips for Brides" 1,865 words
[rest of 20+ story list with titles and word counts is included]

Let me know if you'd like to see any of my work or are interested in purchasing one-time reprint rights to any stories.
Thank you very much for your time; I look forward to hearing from you soon.

Sincerely,
Kelly James-Enger

Note that I highlight the benefits of buying reprint stories to the editor—she can acquire well-written, informative articles at a reasonable price. Note too that I say "purchase reprint rights," so it's clear that I expect to be paid for the articles. (Some magazines offer to print the stories "for the exposure" rather than for money. I prefer the latter.) Finally, I specifically mention "one-time reprint rights" so the editor knows that this article has appeared before—and that she is only purchasing the right to reprint it once. (If you offer rights to an online market, you may want to limit the time the article can appear—say, three or six months. Otherwise it may wind up on the Web forever.)

In other instances, I'll contact a magazine that's new to me and mention that I also have completed articles available in the event their original-article rates are too low for me to consider. Here's an example:

Dear Mr. Jones:

I'm writing to express my interest in writing for Awesome Sports Magazine. I think my background and experience may be a good fit for your publication's needs.

I've been a fulltime freelance journalist for nearly nine years. I specialize in health, fitness, nutrition, and psychology/relationship subjects, and my work has appeared in more than fifty national magazines including Redbook, Self, Health, Muscle Media, American Health & Fitness, Family Circle, Woman's Day, Continental, Fitness, Shape, and Oxygen. I'm also the author of six books including Small Changes, Big Results: A 12-Week Action Plan to a Better Life (Random House, 2005, with Ellie Krieger, R.D.) and am a certified personal trainer.

If your freelance budget is limited, keep in mind that I have dozens of "evergreen" health, fitness, and nutrition stories available on topics that range from the glycemic index to goal-setting to simple stress management techniques. Most articles fall within 500 and 2,000 words, and many include helpful sidebars, quizzes, and other reader-friendly additions. Let me know if you'd like to see my complete story list.

If my skills appear to be a good fit for your publication or others that you produce, I'd love to discuss your editorial needs with you. I'll be happy to send you clips via regular mail if you're interested.

Thank you very much for your time. I look forward to hearing from you soon.

Very truly yours,
Kelly James-Enger

In this case, I didn't know what the market paid, but as a regional publication, I figured the per-word rate for original stories might not be worth my while. This way, I keep the door open for potential reprint sales.

Stay in Touch

As I mentioned, you'll make more from reprints if you sell more than one story at a time. Contacting more than one market at a time is another time-saving strategy. I maintain a "master list" of stories, divided into categories like "nutrition," "fitness," "wellness," and "relationships." I update the list every few months, and send it with a short email to editors who have purchased from me in the past. The hour I spend doing so always results in a few more sales.

For example, I have a market, a regional parenting magazine in California, that buys stories from me occasionally. The magazine only pays between $40 and $65 per story, but my editor always selects a few pieces from my list when I email her. I've sold a dozen pieces to the market in the last four years—for the effort of sending a few emails. As long as your story topic is still relevant and the information it contains still accurate (I do confirm the latter before I send a story out), you can resell the same piece as many times as you like.

Web-based Entrepreneur

There's another way to make money from the articles—or books— you own the rights to. In addition to consulting, Tom Broshahan has radically changed the way he approaches his writing business. Over the years, he'd seen book contracts grow increasingly restrictive, and place more risk on writers. Rather than continuing to write travel guidebooks for traditional publishers, about five years ago he took a year off to write a memoir and then decided to focus on building websites that would replace that income.

"I went cold turkey on traditional print publishing, quit the guidebook-authoring and article-writing I had done for nearly 40 years, and moved most of my work to the Internet," says Brosnahan. "At the start, I had no idea if I could make a living at it. The first few years were difficult, with lots of work and not much money, but now I'm just about back where I was at the height of my print career, earning over six figures."

Brosnahan operates a half-dozen travel websites, including www.Infoexchange.com/, www.TravelInfoExchange.com/, www.TurkeyTravelPlanner.com/, www.StMoritzTravelPlanner.com/, and www.New EnglandTravelPlanner.com/. "I keep all the rights to my work, I have no publisher or editor to deal with, and I publish immediately to the world," he says.

While he has a number of income streams from his web work, much of the money comes from affiliate relationships and click-through advertisements on his sites. It's also enabled him to reach more readers. "My guidebooks gave me a readership of perhaps 100,000 to 125,000 readers per year from perhaps a dozen countries," he says. "My websites give me a readership of 2.25 million from 170 countries."

Of course, making money from the web is more involved than simply slapping up a website and waiting for advertisers to seek you out. Brosnahan spends a lot of time marketing his websites and looking for ways to drive readers to his site. He's responsible for all of the copy, and for framing the information on each web page so that it can easily be found with a search engine. "You have to change your writing style to appeal both to humans and machines," he says. "You salt the keywords in there and if you write pages that way with no tricks and you frame your writing and presentation…and design the content correctly, you can get pretty high in the search engine results."

If you've focused solely on magazine work for years, consider whether it's time to branch out into another field as well. It takes time and effort to try something new, but you may find it an exciting and lucrative way to expand your freelance career.

Money Talks: Maximizing Your Freelance Income

In the previous chapter, you read about several ways to make the most of your specialty, whether through writing books, consulting, or re-selling work. Not only is this a smart use of your time, expanding to other areas can help you survive in a tumultuous freelance market, whether you're a new writer, or have been freelancing for years.

But regardless of experience, I think it's important to believe that you can make a good living as a freelancer. You can make $50,000, $60,000 or even $100,000 a year as a fulltime freelancer, but to do so, you have to approach your writing as a business. That means maximizing your time, negotiating better contracts, developing relationships with editors and other clients, breaking into higher-paying markets, reusing research more than once, and selling reprint rights to stories when possible. For many writers, it means creating one or more specialties as well (hence, this book).

When I started freelancing fulltime in 1997, I grossed just over $17,000, and netted about $11,000—not nearly enough to live on. After four years, though, I was making $70,000 a year; in 2002, I hit the six-figure mark.

Six figures? As a freelancer? It's not impossible, but many writers set their sights too low to make this kind of money. They're also unaware of the work habits and time-saving techniques successful writers employ.

If you want to boost your bottom line or simply work more efficiently, give these 15 strategies a try:

Set a Financial Goal

To make more money as a writer, you have to challenge yourself.

There's nothing wrong with writing for the love of it. But if that's your only goal, you're probably not going to produce a lot of income from your work. Set a financial goal at the beginning of the year, considering the types of writing you're doing and the time you have to devote to it. Be realistic, but give yourself a financial number that you'll have to work to achieve. Simply having that figure in mind will help you reach it.

If you've already been freelancing for some time, consider the kinds of work you're doing, how many steady clients you have, the time you have available to devote to work, and your long-term goals when setting financial goals for the coming year. As you develop relationships with editors and other clients, and become a more efficient writer, you'll probably find that it's easier to make money than your first year or two of freelancing. Or maybe you'll maintain the same financial goal, but allow yourself time to work on other projects (such as a book proposal or even a novel) that don't pay money upfront.

Negotiate for Higher Rates

It's common sense—command a higher rate for the work you're already doing and you'll wind up with more money. But too many writers are afraid to ask for more money when an editor or client offers them work. If this is the case with you, try saying something like, "I'm excited to be working with you, but this story will require a lot of time. Can you boost the fee?" If you've written for the editor before, remind him that he already knows you'll do a good job, and ask if he can sweeten the deal a bit.

"I've never lost an assignment for asking for more money," says Greengard. "I think in the business world, people negotiate fees for everything, and writers should be assertive about asking for more money if they feel they deserve it. The worst that an editor can say is no, and then you have to decide if you want to work on the project."

Pitch Multiple Ideas

Polly Campbell has a long-standing relationship with *The Oregonian*, the statewide newspaper. Rather than pitch stories individually, she sends stories in batches of five or six, which saves both her and editor time—and often, he'll assign all of them. Pitching more than one idea at a time shows editors that you're resourceful, and ups the odds of getting an assignment.

I've used the same approach with magazines I write for regularly. I'll send a letter that includes three to five story ideas, devoting a paragraph to each one. If the editor wants more information about a particular idea, I can provide it, but often a quick paragraph is all I need to net an assignment from someone I've worked with before.

Come up With Spin-offs

Too many writers use a one-idea/one-story approach. Instead, come up with as many spin-off stories as you can from your original idea, and you'll save time and make more money from your initial research. I call these "reslants." A reslant is a story on the same general subject that takes a different angle or approach than the original one; it may or may not use the same sources.

"I revisit my previous stories frequently to see if I can spin them in a different direction. After all, I already have the sources and I've done the research; any subsequent assignments should be fairly easy money," says Rattini. "Sometimes, you might find brand new feature ideas. During an interview with a grocery store owner for *IGA Grocergram*, the man mentioned he was renovating a 100-year-old house into a B&B with the help of the local high school building trades class. I remembered that story, and I pitched it to *This Old House*. They bought it."

Pitch Something New

When you turn in an article, have a new story idea for your editor. By doing so, you'll help ensure a steady flow of work, says Cindrich. "When you pitch a story after working with an editor, the pitch doesn't have to be as formal," says Cindrich. "The query might happen over the phone, via e-mail and appear as a list of ideas you've been thinking about...a quick pitch following a story says 'I'm available...I want to write for you again'."

Another opportune time to pitch your next idea is when an editor contacts you to tell you she's accepting a story. Think about it. She's letting you know that she's happy with your recent work, and she'll never be more favorably disposed toward you than she is at that moment. That's why you should have some story ideas on standby, waiting for this opportunity.

Network With Other Writers

In today's freelance marketplace, networking is more important than ever before. Attend writers' conferences. Participate on writers' bulletin boards. Join writers' organizations. Look for ways that you can help other writers, and you'll quickly start to develop a network of your peers.

"To me, networking is absolutely invaluable. By talking with other writers, you learn about the pay that you can get that maybe you're not getting now, you learn about new markets, about editorial changes, and you can get referred to editors you may have otherwise not encountered," says Bittner. "Other writers can offer you an introduction to an editor you might want to work with. That's been one of my main ways of pitching to new editors, to have a name that I can drop in the first sentence. That's led to assignments and to relationships that I think are going to last a long time."

Look Local

Big magazines pay high rates, but it can take months to get an assignment and finally collect your check. In the meantime, don't overlook business writing projects, which pay decent rates and usually have a much quicker turnaround than magazine work. When I started freelancing, I joined my local chamber of commerce. I quickly picked up three area companies as clients, including a small hospital that needed a writer for press releases and other materials. Over the next year and a half, I billed the hospital between $300 and $1,000 a month for writing services—not bad for a steady gig.

Make sure that your friends and family know you're freelancing; they may be able to hook you up with local companies looking for work. Consider your local newspaper, too—the pay won't be as high as magazines, but the stories are often easy to write and may lead to ideas for magazine pitches as well.

Scout for Reprint Markets

In the last chapter, I pointed out that one of the easiest ways to make money is to resell stories you've already published. The most time-consuming part is finding potential reprint markets, but regional, trade and smaller magazines are all possibilities. Websites may also be interested in purchasing electronic rights to material that's already been published. Keep a lookout for possibilities, and once you find an interested market, update it two or three times a year with newly available stories.

Market, Market, Market

Even when you're swamped with assignments, you should always be scouting for new work. Marketing and writing go hand in hand. "Spend as much time marketing yourself as you spend writing. You should be searching the writing job boards for freelance gigs, contacting editors, reading up about news and changes in the magazine industry, and researching and writing queries," says Formichelli. "Don't think that just because you're busy now you don't need to market yourself. Keeping on top of new markets and job openings will help you keep an even flow of assignments coming in the door."

Focus on the Clock

Writers often focus on the per-word rate they make for stories. Instead, check your per-hour rate. For example, if you're assigned a 1,000-word story at 75 cents per word and it takes you 10 hours to write it, that's an hourly rate of $75 per hour. A 1,000-word article at $1 per word sounds like a better deal, but if it turns out that you spend 20 hours on it, you're making only $50 per hour. Don't be distracted by the per-word rate—figure out how much time it's likely to take before you accept an assignment. You may find that lower-paying markets produce a better hourly rate because they take less time to produce.

"After a while, you have a pretty good idea of how long a project is going to take and if you can't work within those parameters then you have to decide whether you want to take it anyway for some other reason than the money," says Greengard. "There are times when I'll work for 50 cents a word or 30 cents a word because I can make $500 or $1,000 for an hour's work; there are other times when I don't want to touch a project that pays $3 a word because I'm going to spend weeks or months being put through the meat grinder."

Forget the Muse

Treat your writing business like a business, not a hobby. "Discipline is more important than inspiration, I think," says Sena. "Treat deadlines seriously. Send invoices promptly. I see a lot of beginning writers talking about waiting for 'the muse.' I believe that just keeping a regular writing schedule will help you produce far more good writing than you'll ever create by sitting around waiting for a spark of inspiration. That doesn't sound terribly romantic, but it leads to more published articles and more checks in the mail."

Keep Detailed Records

There's another significant reason to approach your writing like a business instead of a hobby. Once you're writing for money instead of love alone, the IRS lets you take your writing-related expenses as business tax deductions. Demonstrating a "profit motive" with your writing is the first step. Keep records of your queries and submissions, and track your income and expenses. The more legitimate expenses you can deduct from your gross income, the less you'll net—and that means less taxes and more in your pocket at the end of the year.

Build Relationships

Writing is like any other job—you need to build relationships with people. "A good editor should be cultivated like any other good client. I talk to my editors a lot," says Campbell. "I don't waste their time, but I take any opportunity to talk to them in person, whether it's a visit or a phone call. The other thing is I try to understand their job situations so I know when their deadlines are, and I make it clear that I know that. I show respect for their time."

In fact, successful freelancers know how to keep their editors happy. "My editors like me because I never miss a deadline, I turn in clean copy (no spelling or grammar mistakes, no awkward phrasing), and when they ask for changes, I do them," says Harper. "I sometimes argue with changes, or course, but the bottom line is this: the editor is the boss. If I don't like the way an editor is handling a story, I still give the editor what he or she wants on that story. I might not work with him or her again, but on every assignment from that editor, I try to give him or her what she wants."

Streamline the Process

If you know you're good at a certain type of writing—say service journalism pieces or round-ups—do more of them to boost your income. "By specializing, I've gotten 'as-told-tos' [first-person true-life features] down to an art," says Newsome. "They only require one source and I can practically write these stories in my sleep so I get paid a lot of money for relatively little time. I've also learned what works, what doesn't and why, so I don't waste a lot of time with proposals that don't go anywhere. That's a big plus."

"I think the main reason successful writers are successful is that they are fast," agrees Harper. "This is something they don't usually tell you in book or at conferences. Freelancers who make a living at it are efficient and productive. That means more than being motivated or disciplined. It means cranking the stuff out. The more you finish, the more you sell, the more money you make."

Believe in Yourself

And finally, don't overlook your attitude. "You have to be self-confident and believe that you can do the job. I run into a lot of writers who just don't think their work is worth appearing in a national magazine or it's only worth a $1/word or they wouldn't dream of touching a contract," says Bittner. "If you're confident in your abilities and in yourself, you will seek what your work is worth, you will step up to better paying markets, you will negotiate contracts and ultimately you will be a more successful freelancer, regardless of how you define success."

And that is my hope for you—success as a freelancer, however you define it. Whatever you decide to specialize in, I wish you lots of assignments and a fulfilling career!

Appendix - Resources

There's no shortage of excellent resources out there for freelancers. I've included some of my favorites below.

Books

Book writing/authorship

Damn! Why Didn't I Write That? How Ordinary People are Raking in $100,000.00...or more Writing Nonfiction Books & How You Can Too!
Mark McCutcheon (Quill Driver, 2001)
Includes some great advice on finding an underserved audience and catching editors' and readers' attention with your book

The Forest for the Trees
Betsy Lerner (Riverhead, 2001)
Fascinating, funny, and full of anecdotes about the real world of book publishing

How to Write a Book Proposal
Michael Larsen (Writer's Digest Books, 1997)
Excellent how-to guide with plenty of practical advice

Jeff Herman's Guide to Book Publishers, Editors and Agents 2008
Jeff Herman (Three Dog Press, 2008)
The scoop on hundreds of publishers, editors and agents

Nonfiction Book Proposals Anybody Can Write: How to Get a Contract and Advance before Writing your Book
Elizabeth Lyon and Natasha Kern (Perigree, 2002)
Another excellent book; I used both Larsen's and Lyon's books to write my first book proposals

Write the Perfect Book Proposal: 10 Proposals that Sold and Why
Michael Larsen (John Wiley and Sons, 1993)
Includes 10 actual book proposals

Resources

Business writing/copywriting

The Copywriter's Handbook
Robert Bly (Henry Holt, 1990)
Somewhat outdated but good basic info on getting ready to write, writing print ads, direct mail, writing to communicate, sell, etc.

Persuading on Paper: The Complete Guide to Writing Copy that Pulls in Business
Marcia Yudkin (Plume, 1996)
Good overview; includes information on basic layout, different formats, and working with printers and graphic designers

The Well-Fed Writer: Financial Self-Sufficiency as a Freelance Writer in Six Months or Less
Peter Bowerman (Fanove Publishing, 2000)
Good overview of writing for corporations and business; lots of practical suggestions and samples; includes how to freelance fulltime, find clients, sell yourself and the like

Magazine writing

How to Write Irresistible Query Letters
Lisa Collier Cool (F & W, 2002)
Nuts and bolts on the all-important queries, with plenty of examples

The Renegade Writer: A Totally Unconventional Guide to Freelance Writing Success
Linda Formichelli and Diana Burrell (Marion Street Press, 2003)
Helpful examination of the "rules" of magazine writing and when and why you should break them

The Renegade Writer's Query Letters That Rock
Linda Formichelli and Diana Burrell (Marion Street Press, 2006)
Samples of query letters that sold—and an explanation of why

You Can Write for Magazines
Greg Daugherty (Writer's Digest Books, 1999)
Pretty good guide for beginners, practical tips and suggestions

Market Resources

Bacon's Magazine Directory and Bacon's Newspaper Directory
(Primedia Information Inc., 2007)
Published annually, Bacon's includes 70,000 magazines and newspapers, divided into subject headings

Gale Directory of Publications and Broadcast Media, 140th Edition
(Gale Group, 2007)
This multi-volume series is updated annually and includes over 54,500 newspapers, magazines, journals and other periodicals, subdivided by city and state

The Standard Periodical Directory
(Oxbridge Communications, 2007)
Also published annually, the *SPD* lists more than 75,000 U.S. and Canadian publications by subject

Writer's Market 2007 (updated annually)
Robert Lee Brewer, editor (Writer's Digest Books, 2006)
Popular market guide; includes rate information and how-to pieces

Running Your Writing Business

The ASJA Guide to Freelance Writing
Timothy Harper, editor (St. Martin's Griffin, 2003)
Excellent overview of issues facing fulltime and part-time freelancers

J.K. Lasser's Taxes Made Easy for Your Home-based Business, Fifth Edition
Gary W. Carter (John Wiley & Sons, 2002)
Good "plain English" guide to what you need to know about taxes, deductions, and the like

Six-Figure Freelancing: The Writer's Guide to Making More Money
Kelly James-Enger (Random House, 2005)
Want more from me? Six-Figure Freelancing shows you how to set up your writing business, work more efficiently, and develop relationships with editors and clients; includes templates

The Writer's Legal Companion: The Complete Handbook for the Working Writer, Third Edition
Brad Bunnin and Peter Beren (Perseus, 1998)
Legal advice for freelancers

The Writer's Legal Guide: An Authors Guild Desk Reference, Third Edition
Tad Crawford and Kay Murray (Allworth Press, 2002)
More legal advice for freelancers

Organizations/Web Resources

American Society of Journalists and Authors
1501 Broadway, Suite 302
New York, NY 10036
Phone: 212-997-0947
Fax: 212-778-7414
Web: www.asja.org
This 1,100-member organization consists of nonfiction writers, most of whom are freelancers. $195/year; I've found it worth the money for the contract and rate info members can access.

Authors Guild
31 E. 28th St.
New York, NY 10016
Phone: 212-563-5904
Fax: 212-564-5363
Web: www.authorsguild.org
This 8,100-member organization consists of professional book and magazine writers. First year dues, $90. Offers health, hospitalization, dental and life insurance to members.

Cassell Network of Writers/Writers-Editors Network
www.writers-editors.com
Members have access to market info, publishing updates, and other information; basic membership $39/year.

Freelance Success
www.freelancesuccess.com
Freelance Success includes a weekly email newsletter with detailed market reports; members have access to an onsite bulletin board. $89/year; great resource.

National Writers Union
113 University Place, 6th Floor
New York, NY 10003-4527
Phone: 212-254-0279
Fax: 212-254-0673
Web: www.nwu.org

The NWU consists of freelance writers, journalists, authors and other writers. $95-260/year. Offers health insurance to NY-based members.

About the Author

Kelly James-Enger escaped from the law in 1997, but don't worry—she's no fugitive. Since then, the former attorney has launched a successful freelance career, writing for more than 50 national magazines including *Redbook, Health, Self, Woman's Day, Parents,* and *Continental.* She is also the author of six books including *Six-Figure Freelancing: The Writer's Guide to Making More Money* (Random House, 2005), *Live it Up! 50 Cool, Unique, and Worthwhile Ways to Spend your Time* (Random House, 2007), *Small Changes, Big Results: A 12-Week Action Plan to a Better Life* (with Ellie Krieger, R.D., Random House, 2005), and the novels *Did You Get the Vibe?* (Strapless, 2003) and *White Bikini Panties* (Strapless, 2004).

James-Enger also speaks on topics ranging from fitness, nutrition, and health/wellness to writing (both for fun and profit), time management, stress management, and finding the strength to pursue your dreams. She's known as an entertaining, inspiring motivational speaker and has spoken at dozens of events throughout the country, addressing audiences as small as six to as large as 700, customizing her topic and presentation for each audience. She's the owner of BodyWise Consulting, a business which shares practical, real-life fitness, nutrition, and wellness information with a variety of audiences, and lives outside Chicago with her husband, son, and golden retriever. She can be reached at Kelly@becomebodywise.com. Visit her website, www.becomebodywise.com, to sign up for Writer's Gear, a free monthly newsletter to help you succeed in your freelance writing career.

Index